THE EVOLUTION OF V

A WOMAN'S INCREDIBLE JOURNEY TO REDEMPTION AND VICTORY

Victoria M Howard

authorHOUSE®

AuthorHouse™
1663 Liberty Drive
Bloomington, IN 47403
www.authorhouse.com
Phone: 1 (800) 839-8640

Holy Bible, New International Version®, NIV® Copyright ©1973, 1978, 1984, 2011 by Biblica, Inc.® Used by permission. All rights reserved worldwide.

Published by AuthorHouse 08/15/2018

ISBN: 978-1-5462-5548-2 (sc)
ISBN: 978-1-5462-5547-5 (e)

Library of Congress Control Number: 2018909709

Print information available on the last page.

To my family in Christ: Paula, Wayne, Ron, Wes, Colleen and Lyndell.

Contents

PREFACE

This book was not written to judge, be judged, ridicule, or try to convert anyone. Every one has the right to choose what they believe and the way they want to live their life.

This is not just for Christians but is a non-fiction unlike any you have ever read.

Some people question what the reason for our existence is or how we actually came to be, but those who are believers know the answer.

Unfortunately, there is no physical way to illustrate the evidence of God's existence, but there are many facts surrounding God's existence. Such as: **The complexity of our planet**, which points to a designer who not only created the universe, but sustains it today. The Earth is located the right distance from the sun, for any closer we would burn up.

1.) **The existence of water**.
   It is colorless, tasteless, yet, no living thing can survive without it.

2.) **The human brain**.
   This organ possesses an amazing amount of information. The brain takes in colors and objects we see, the temperature around you, the dryness in your mouth and processes all your emotions, thoughts and memories.

These are just a few of the many facts that should prove the existence of God. But some may still ask, "Does God really exist?"

We know God exists because:

1) He performed many miracles during His walk on earth that thousands witnessed.

2) He still is performing miracles today in your life and mine.

3) He is constantly initiating and seeking for us to come to Him.

God does not force us to believe in Him, although He could. Instead, He has proven time and time again, responsive to those of us in our hours of need. He only counsels, "Believe."

(*Names have been changed to protect certain individual's privacy.)

A WORD FROM THE AUTHOR

THE EVOLUTION OF V is a story that some could personally relate to. As you're reading it you may say, "That sounds like me", or "That's happened to me."

It's a true story of a woman who was spiritually lost and lived her life in the dark like far too many do while battling personal demons. She was constantly searching for that one thing or person she *thought* could bring her what was missing in her life-- true love and perpetual peace.

Throughout her intoxicating life she looked to men, material things and fame thinking it was the missing link that would fill the emptiness that lingered inside her since childhood. But alas, it would always end the same painstakingly way--- heartbreak and alone.

Her vulnerability and sensitive heart opened the door to evil and darkness. It did not always appear in human form but through fame, beauty, power, and material things. No matter how much or what she acquired there was always emptiness that remained within.

After two painful divorces, the loss of most of her finances, and inflicted with a serious health issue, her life turned upside down and she found herself facing her demons alone.

Questioning the decisions she made in her life, she fell to the ground and surrendered for she could not do it on her own anymore.

Finally after hitting rock bottom she discovered the missing link. To her surprise the answer had been right in front of her all the time.

The woman I am talking about is me, and by the grace of God I am here to tell this story. There are parts you may question for even I find certain events hard to believe. But I guarantee you these things took place.

People say I have lived an extraordinary life and I guess I have. I'm not special; it's just that God allowed me to go through these supernatural, ambiguous situations for a reason.

After years of questioning Him, praying, and being

chastened, I discovered the answer. It was to write this book and tell my story to help others find the way to peace and happiness. The answer was amazingly simple--there is only one way and that is through our savior Jesus Christ.

Victoria

John 14:6 *"Jesus answered, I am the way and the truth and the life. No one comes to the Father except through me."*

1   My First Heartbreak

Back in the 50's divorce rate in America was in the twenty percentile. Today, at least fifty per cent of marriages end in divorce, regardless of any religious indoctrination.

There are innumerable and profound reasons for the rapid increase, but for whatever reason the union dissolves those who usually suffer most are the children. Unfortunately, I also was a victim of a broken marriage.

******

The year was 1958.

I was a fragile four-year-old girl. It's funny, I can't remember what I ate for dinner yesterday but that rainy night in October 1958, I recall like it was yesterday.

I was lying on the living room floor with my daddy watching The Three Stooges waiting for my mother to come home from work.

When she walked in the front door I immediately sensed something wasn't right. She told my dad a taxi was outside waiting for she was leaving him and taking me with her.

I vividly remember daddy holding my one arm and

mom holding the other. It was an exceptionally dark and dreary night and the rain was coming down in torrents.

Abruptly my mother and I left our "white house" as I called it; the one place I felt truly secure.

Daddy was in shock begging her not to take me away but her mind was adamant. I was whisked into the yellow cab and I never saw that house again.

But please don't think ill of my mother. She was a wonderful, loving woman who lived and breathed for her baby girl.

There are generally two sides to every story.

My parents were both quite young when they married--- maybe too young--- as people wed earlier back then.

Daddy was a famous musician who played trumpet in a jazz band. Because of his exceptional good looks he had his share of groupies lining up to meet him every night.

Mother was drop dead gorgeous. Daddy used to love telling me the story about the first time he saw her. He was at a club playing music when this beautiful raven-haired teenager sauntered in. He turned to the drummer and said, "I'm going to marry that girl someday."

And he did.

Whatever the real reason was that led to the dissolution of their marriage went to their graves with them, as neither ever discussed it with me.

******

After my parents divorce daddy would pick me up on Sundays, which was his designated day. Since he had no idea how to handle a five-year-old girl, he took me to his sister's house.

Those days are some of my fondest memories for visiting my aunt and cousins simulated a real family to me.

For the next few years I was tossed like a hot potato from one person to another. I now believe that the absence of my father at that tender age was the start of what would become a lifelong quest for finding the "father figure."

This lapse of a parental role eventually manifested into a thoroughly dysfunctional pattern of seeking the wrong men, which dominated the majority of my adult life.

During the next five decades I would meet every type of Mr. Wrong known to womanhood.

Malachi 2:16 *"The man who hates and divorces his wife," says the Lord, the God of Israel, "does violence to the one he should protect."*

2 Those Turbulent Teenage Years

Growing up in the swinging sixties will be remembered because of the fall or relaxation of social taboos.

It was during the sixties that the Woodstock Festival took place in upstate New York and psychedelic drugs were introduced and widely used--- medicinally, spiritually and recreationally.

It was also a time of revolution and change in politics when on January 20, 1961 John F. Kennedy became the thirty-fifth president of the United States and was assasinated on November 22, 1963.

The music world would make history when four young men called The Beatles who came from Liverpool introduced unconventional recording techniques, becoming the foremost and most influential music band in history.

It was during the sixties when sex, drugs, and rock-and-roll thrived. Some called it "the decade of discontent" because of the demonstrations against the war and the race riots.

Others called it "the decade of peace and harmony" because of the peace movement and the emergence of "the flower child" syndrome.

During that time you could safely leave your front door unlocked and children played outside until dusk. Although there was some violence, it was at a much smaller degree. You didn't turn television on and hear about children abductions, rapes, and murders on a daily basis.

Television shows like Ozzie and Harriet, Flipper, and The Brady Bunch were popular as the entire family gathered to watch while munching popcorn.

In 1968 my mother enrolled me in the prestigious Barbizon Modeling School to learn proper etiquette and poise.

Since I was on the tall, slender side, I fit the physical requirements of a model.

One day the school informed me I was one of the girls chosen to audition to be the new "Chiquita Banana" girl. The original was Carmen Miranda, the Brazilian actress who wore a fruit-basket headdress and long flowing two-piece dress, revealing her abdomen.

The following day mom drove me downtown for the interview. She was told to wait in the lobby while the man in charge interviewed me.

As we were arriving another mother and daughter were leaving. I assumed the girl was also there for the job. She was a pretty girl around thirteen but appeared much older for she wore bright red lipstick and a lot of rouge on her cheeks.

I, on the other hand was bare faced, for my mother forbid me to even apply colored lipgloss.

I noticed the girl had been crying for her make-up had run down her face and wondered why she was so upset.

Mother said she most likely didn't get the job and the reason she was crying

When it was my turn to be interviewed I nervously walked into the room. As soon as the door closed the man said, "You are my pick. I think you would make a perfect Chiquita Banana girl, but first you have to show me your breasts!"

I was shocked for in my thirteen years of living on the planet nobody ever said that to me or even suggested such a thing!

I now knew why that girl had been crying. She had either showed him her breasts or like myself refused. Of course neither one of us got the job!

When I told my mother what had happened she called the man who of course denied ever saying that. That was my first experience in discovering looks and sex could get certain girls a lot of things and go places others could only dream about.

******

Ever since I learned to walk, I loved to dance.

I took ballet, tap, jazz, and acrobatic lessons and loved them all.

But what I really liked was to go to the seventies record hops where the twist, mashed potato, and the Watusi were the raves. What a great way to keep in shape.

When I was sixteen my girlfriend and I attended an exotic automobile show that was also hosting a go-go contest. These were the days when the television show, Laugh In was popular and Goldie Hawn danced in a cage.

Just for the fun of it my girlfriend Kim and I tried out, never expecting to get very far. But to my surprise, when the auditions were over I was asked to come back the following night for the finals.

I was stunned for I had never engaged in any type of go-go dancing as did the other contestants--- some of who were paid professionals and much older than I was.

I ran home and told my mother I was chosen as one of the finalists so the following day she took me shopping to buy an outfit for the competition for I had no proper dancing attire.

That evening my family accompanied me to the venue and watched the dancers compete. The place was packed, mostly with young men who came to see the hot rods and sexy go-go dancers.

When it was my time to dance a lot of wolf whistles came from the audience, infuriated my step-father, but mother informed him he didn't need to worry for they were there to protect me.

At the end of the night after the points were totaled, to everybody's surprise they announced I came in second place.

******

Two weeks later I received a phone call from the owners of the contest informing me I actually didn't finish in second place, but had tied for first. I earned the exact number of points as the winner but since she was a renowned dancer on the circuit and a veteran in that field they awarded her the title of "Miss Pittsburgh A-Go-Go."

However, I was designated the title of "Miss Greater

Pittsburgh A-Go-Go" and would compete in "The Miss USA A-Go-Go Pageant" held in New York City.

In November I flew to the Big Apple with my family in tow----winning a multitude of trophies. I won the title of "Best Figure" and "Miss Girl Watcher 1970" which was voted by the audience.

What a heady experience for a sixteen-year-old girl.

******

I had never been anywhere outside my hometown and New York City was insane. The busy streets were filled with pretty models all waiting to be discovered.

The store windows on Fifth Avenue displayed the newest fashions.

It was Thanksgiving week so we got to see the Macy's Day Parade. I felt truly blessed to be able to experience this with my family in tow.

During the day the dancers got paid for modeling by the fancy cars and at night the dance contest would be held live in front of hundreds of people.

The New York Times sent a photographer to select one girl to pose in Bob Hope's custom-made golf cart. The vehicle had a huge nose just like Mr. Hopes. I was chosen and appeared on the front cover of The New York Times posing in the car.

I got more than my share of passes from the men in the audience not realizing I was only sixteen, as by then I could pass for much older. Fortunately, my mother intervened any possible sticky situation by telling one and all that they were wasting their time for I was "jailbait." But I can't deny I loved all the attention.

When I returned from New York I received a call from a local television station inviting me to audition as a go-go dancer on a weekly dance show. It was similar to American Bandstand, where teenagers would dance to live bands.

I auditioned and got the job.

Every Saturday I was one of two dancers who performed on a five-foot wooden drum that acted as a stage. Tanya, my dance partner, was a beautiful twenty-six-year old who was not only a professional dancer but I would soon discover was a "pro" at another career. (Ironically, she was also the dancer I tied with in the local contest)

Tanya and I would meet at her apartment every week and incorporate a routine to dance to on the next show.

Since I wasn't old enough to have a driver's license mom would have to drive me and pick me up a few hours later.

While we were rehearsing, Tanya would stop every so often to answer the phone. At that time I never understood why she received so many calls. She would tell the caller her roommate Susie wasn't there and asked if she could do?

I thought to myself "do what?" I was beyond innocent at that time.

When I told my mother about the calls she refused to bring me to Tanya's house and insisted she come to ours.

One week a rock band whose record was #1 appeared on the show. While I was preparing for our first routine, Tanya disappeared in the dressing room with the drummer. When the manager asked me to get her I discovered my dancing partner naked up against the wall, with the musician.

On the dressing table I noticed numerous lines of a white substance, which I later discovered was something called cocaine.

That was my initial introduction into drugs.

******

It was during this time that I met a young man named Joe who was seven years my senior. He became my first 'real' boyfriend.

I was a senior in high school and Joe was attending Pitt University Law School. Up until then I had never been intimate with a boy before. He would be my first.

My stepfather (who my mother married when I was four years old) had gotten involved with horse racing and just bought a racehorse.

Joe and I would occasionally visit the stables and groom the horse. Within a few months the three of us put our money together and purchased a four-year-old Standardbred mare, named Who Du Girl.

I fell madly in love with the horse and decided not to attend college for I wanted to make horseracing my career.

One day Joe and I drove our horse trailer to my great-uncles tire shop for it needed new tires. While I was waiting in his office, Uncle Bill came up behind me and put his hands down my shirt and fondled my breasts. I couldn't believe what he was doing, but luckily Joe walked in and my uncle fled the room.

When I got home and told mother I discovered that Uncle Bill did the same thing to her and her sister when they were about my age.

I never understood how a family member could make sexual advances towards his own niece? To this day I still can't fathom how the incident was ignored by some of the family members; but that act of betrayal was unfortunately something I would encounter periodically throughout my life.

******

When I was eighteen Joe and I moved into an apartment together. My strict Catholic upbringing preached you didn't have sex until you married. I was told that intercourse without marriage showed disrespect for the sacrament of marriage-- the sacredness of sex and human dignity.

Mom used to say, "Why would a man buy a cow when he can get the milk free?"

This left a bad taste in my mouth that perhaps men just wanted a woman for what he could get sexually, and why would he marry a woman when sex without a commitment was so easy?

******

I never told my mom I was living with Joe and she never once came over to visit, perhaps choosing to believe the lie I told her--- that I was living with a girlfriend. I guess deep down inside she knew, but didn't want to admit it.

Although I had a nagging feeling what I was doing was wrong, I loved Joe and thought we would be together forever.

But it wasn't easy sneaking around making sure our parents didn't discover we were living in sin. We had two separate phone lines installed in our apartment---each with a different number. One was strictly for my family, so I was the only one who could answer it, and the other was for Joe.

To help pay the house bills, I took a part time job as a 'shoeshine girl' at an upscale men's barbershop in a ritzy part of town. It really was an easy job. All I had to do was buff and shine the men's shoes and for my services I was generously tipped.

My boss liked me and supplied a full calendar— sometimes I had 6 or 8 customers in one day. The only thing he asked was that I would wear a tight or low cut blouse.

I wasn't comfortable with this request, but Joe assured me that was the reason I was bringing home a couple hundred dollars a day.

Remember, this was during the early seventies and back then that was good money for a young girl who did nothing but polish shoes.

******

My boss said there was someone he wanted me to meet. His name was Jim and he looked like the actor Steve McQueen. Jim lived in Atlanta, Georgia, and stopped in to have his hair cut every month when he was in town on business.

One morning after I had been working at the salon for several weeks in walks a handsome, tall man who could have been Steve McQueen's double. Instinctively I said, "You must be Jim."

It turned out that Jim was a trust fund baby whose father founded the largest elevator company in the world.

That day Jim took me to lunch and asked why I was working at a men's barbershop shining shoes. He asked me what I really wanted to do with my life and without hesitation I replied, "I've always wanted to be a Playboy Bunny."

When we finished lunch we returned to the barbershop where Jim made a phone call to the Atlanta Playboy Club for the manager was a good friend of his. He set up an interview the following week and made my airline reservations.

When I got home and told Joe what happened, I was surprised to see that he totally supported it. He said he knew this was my dream and didn't want to be the one who stood between it. The next week Joe drove me to the airport, gave me a kiss, and wished me luck.

******

When I got off the plane, Jim was waiting in a bright yellow Lamborghini Miura SV. I had never seen anything so beautiful (and fast) in my life.

He drove me to his house, (or should I say mansion) located in a very ritzy part of town.

As I entered his home I noticed a picture hanging on the living room wall of Jim's father standing next to the President of the United States. It was obvious that Jim came from a very wealthy and powerful family.

He gave me a tour of his magnificent home and said, "You can stay in the main bedroom upstairs. If you want privacy, lock the door. Here is the key." And that's exactly what I did.

The following day Jim took me to the Atlanta Playboy Club where I was fitted for the signature bunny suit. I was excited, yet a little anxious, for this was all happening so fast.

As I sat in the foyer waiting to meet the club manager, I was in awe of all the beautiful young women prancing around in their provocative uniforms. One woman was prettier than the next and all appeared to be enjoying what they were doing.

It was lunchtime and there were a lot of businessmen sitting at the bar, some dining, while others were having a drink, talking to one of the Bunny's.

After my fitting and interview I was informed that I got the job. The manager introduced me to the Bunny Mother and several of the gorgeous Bunny's who worked there. The Bunny Mother, Miss Kelly, welcomed me to their family and informed me I would start in two weeks.

During the drive back to Jim's house I was quiet, absorbing all that was happening to me. He looked over, smiled, grabbed my hand and said, "When you move here, I will set you up in your own apartment and car. You won't have to worry about a thing."

Later that night I overheard Jim talking on the phone to his father. He said, "Dad, I want you to come visit soon, for there's someone I'd like you to meet. Her name is Vicki and she is going to be my next wife."

Jim didn't know I was in the other room and heard his conversation. Although he had been a gentleman, I knew that 'setting me up with my own apartment and car' meant he expected a lot more than just friendship.

A few minutes after he hung up I walked into the room and told him I wasn't feeling well. I excused myself, went to the bedroom, locked the door and didn't come out until the following morning when it was time to catch the plane.

At the airport Jim gave me a friendly kiss and said, "I'll see you in two weeks, honey. I can't wait until you come back."

As soon as I returned home I changed my phone number, quit my job, and never talked to Jim again. And I never took the job as a bunny.

1 **John 2:16** *"For all that is in the world—the desires of the flesh and the desires of the eyes and pride of life—is not from the Father but is from the world."*

3 The Crazy Twenties

The saying "being in the right place at the right time" is so true.

Throughout the years there's been movies stars and celebrities who were discovered at the most unusual places.

Lana Turner was at a Hollywood and Vine Malt shop enjoying a malt, Charlize Theron was spotted arguing with a bank teller in a South African bank and Pamela Anderson was attending a B.C. Lions football game dressed in a tight cut-off Labatt blue t-shirt, which earned her a few seconds of fame on the stadium's Jumbo Tron. That was enough time to get her numerous offers for modeling-- and the rest is history.

Actress Natalie Portman was having pizza in a pizza parlor when an executive for Revlon spotted her and asked if she had any interest in becoming a model. She replied, "I would rather act than model" and was signed up with a talent agency.

Nothing exciting like that happened to me, but when I was nineteen attending a friend's wedding, the photographer approached and asked if I would let him take pictures of me for a men's magazine.

At first I thought this was a creepy suggestion but after Joe verified that the man was indeed a legitimate photographer who had shot many Playboy Magazine centerfolds, he encouraged me to let him take them.

Up until that time I had appeared in numerous fashion magazines but was always fully clothed.

A few weeks later Marc (the photographer) came to my apartment and snapped several dozen photos. I had never modeled topless before, but since Joe was permitted to remain in the room I felt more at ease.

After the rolls were sent in and viewed by the editor of the magazine I received a phone call asking me to fly to their headquarters in Chicago.

The next month I flew to Chicago where I was photographed by photographer, Stan Malinowski. The photo shots were more suggestive than the first set done in my home, but Stan was a total gentleman and made me feel as comfortable as possible.

I knew of Mr. Malinowski's work having been in the modeling world and knew he was one of the best photographer's in the field. His work graced the covers of Vogue, Bazaar, Playboy and Penthouse; and he photographed Christie Brinkley, Cindy Crawford and Isabella Rosselini. I was honored that this famous cameraman was photographing me, although I would never be in the ranks that these supermodels were.

When the photo shoot was over, I flew back home.

Two weeks later I received a phone call from a man in New York informing me he had just purchased the magazine, Gallery, and would be re-naming it.

He said his name was Larry and he loved my photos and would like to use them in the first issue (the debut edition, aka/ the collector's issue) of the new magazine.

He invited me to New York to meet him for he met all his models. Of course, I didn't go.

Larry called me several times informing me he loved my pictures and was not only using them for the magazine but was going to place one in his bedroom. After he told me that I started questioning his credibility and reason for pursuing me.

One of the stipulations of my posing was I would have the opportunity to look over the photos and approve which ones would be used, *before* they were published. But alas, that never happened.

After several weeks the incessant phone calls ceased. Two months later a friend of mine called saying he bought the first issue and inside was an eight-page pictorial spread of me.

I was enraged! I never got to see my pictures to approve which ones could be published and never got paid for them!

A short time after the magazine was put on the stands the New York Police called me inquiring how I knew the owner of the magazine and what our relationship was. I informed them I never met Larry and only talked on the phone to him several times.

Apparently, the police got my phone number from his phone bill, as they were investigating all the numbers on it.

It appeared someone had just shot him and he was in critical condition.

From that calamitous experience I learned a lot about people, shady business deals, and "You reap what you sow!"

My mother knew nothing of my posing nude. She was humiliated and embarrassed that I posed naked for pictures in a magazine where millions of people could see them and didn't talk to me for one year.

At that time I thought I wanted that kind of notoriety, but in the end all it got me was shame, trouble, and broke my mother's heart---- which would haunt me the rest of my life.

******

After the magazine episode the next five years of my life was pretty ordinary. I married Joe and two years later we had a beautiful baby boy.

I tried to settle into a normal, happy family life. Although getting married and becoming a mother was something I always wanted that empty void still lingered inside.

After I gave birth to my son, I brought him to work with me every day. At that time I was working at a horse stable with my husband and thought by keeping our family together would solidify it.

I desperately tried to make my marriage work, for I didn't want my son, Joey, to endure what I had when my parents divorced. I swore I would do whatever it took to stay married, but things happen that are sometimes beyond one's ability to change.

Later in life when I was in therapy, the doctor told me

I sustained the behavioral pattern seen in many peoples' marriages, for children learn from their parents who are their first teachers.

Developmental psychologists say that children assimilate by imitating adults. For example, if a child sees his parents fighting this is what he comes to know as 'familiar.' If a child is sexually abused, there is good chance that he or she will grow up to be a sexual abuser!

******

By the time my son turned five years old, Joe and I began drifting apart. I pleaded with him to go with me and see a marriage counselor, but being the stubborn man he was, he refused.

Maybe our marriage ended because he was no longer getting the attention he once got, or perhaps it was the fact that he was my first and only boyfriend and we were now evolving at different rates of speed.

After my divorce I moved back home with my mother and stepfather who opened their arms and home to my son and me.

A short time later I began seeing someone I had known for years. His name was John and he was sixteen years my senior. Once again, I was seeking that 'father figure' to protect and love me.

Galatians 6:7-8 *"Do not be deceived: God is not mocked, for whatever one sows, that he will also reap."*

4   The Painful Thirties

I was in my early thirties when I married the second time.

He was "the man of my dreams," and to this day I can honestly say the o*nly* man I truly ever *romantically* loved.

John was a successful businessman and self-made millionaire who came from humble origins. I never knew a man who had more drive and ambition than he had.

He had been married twice before but both unions dissolved because of his working 24/7. Seeing what the problem was I thought if I couldn't beat him I'd join him so I went to work with John every day as his personal assistant. You didn't see one of us without the other.

My friends would ask how I could stand to be constantly with him. The answer was simple--he was my best friend, my husband, my partner and my lover.

When I married John he came with baggage--- five children—the oldest five years younger than I was. I was thrilled that my son, Joey, being an only child would have older brothers and sisters.

For the next five years my husband and I worked very hard together and built an empire. There was nothing I didn't have. I had two closets full of designer clothes, fancy cars, sparkling diamonds and even a mansion on the hill.

Despite having it all that nagging emptiness I felt inside ever since I was a little child lingered.

"Why couldn't I be happy? I had everything in the world. That is, everything material—but spiritually, I was barren.

John used to say that nothing could make me happy. I heard this for years and to tell you the truth, he was right.

It's sad to look back now and realize what was missing. If I only knew the answer then our marriage might have survived.

During our marriage neither one of us attended church. We were non-practicing Catholics who never gave credit for our success and wealth to God. But I now know that no matter what religion we had practiced without the Holy Spirit in our lives our marriage was destined for failure.

******

It was during the sixth year of marriage that we began having problems. Having gone through this before, I knew the signs to look for.

It was a pattern that continued from my parents failed marriage into mine. The belittling, the name calling, the emotional abuse my mother endured from my dad continued into my marriage. I knew this dysfunctional behavior as "familiar" for as I said children observe how their parents interact and view this as normal.

The emotional abuse was something I deemed as

routine, thus when I married and my husband began verbally abusing me, I viewed it as a standard way of married life.

I was determined not to go through yet another divorce and began looking at myself as a failure.

John, like my first husband Joe, refused to go to a marriage counselor so I began seeing a therapist on my own.

The doctor prescribed an anti-depressant that seemed to work for a while. I called it "my happy pill" for it gave me energy, false happiness, and the impression that things would get better.

I had been on the meds for several months when I had my first panic attack. I was on an airplane and couldn't catch my breath when I started to freak and broke out in a cold sweat. I did everything I could to contain myself from pushing the emergency button and summon the stewardess. I sat on my hands, prayed and asked God to help me, and He did.

When I returned home I went back to the doctors and told her about my attack. She changed the medication to another one, but nothing ever solved the problem.

Medication is necessary at times, but in my case it was just a 'quick fix.' The meds were a bandage, covering a deep scab that eventually would re-open and bleed. Then it was on to a new medicine, and so on and so on. I now know that the *best* and *only* medicine that could have cured my ailment was the Holy Spirit living inside me.

******

The first few years of my second marriage was "as good as it gets." Of course, there were turbulent times, for every marriage has them.

Although I had known John a few years before marrying him I never knew he had a mental illness for he hid it well.

For the first two years John apparently was going through one of his stable phases for he appeared normal.

One day when he awoke he buried himself under the covers saying he wanted to die! Panicking and not knowing what was happening I drove him to the hospital where his doctor informed me he was 'cycling.'

He explained that my husband was a manic-depressant and had been since birth and assured me with the proper medication the disease could be controlled.

He explained the disease is dubbed "the common cold of mental health" and affects about 2.5% of the adult population in the U.S. today.

People who are bi-polar experience frequent mood swings.

When they are in the manic stage, known as extreme elation, they are out of control and behave wildly.

It affects people in different ways. Some excessively spend or gamble money they don't have. Some abuse alcohol or drugs, while others sleep around with anyone and everyone that is available to them at the time.

When bi-polar people are in the depressed phase they feel sad and hopeless and may even have thoughts of suicide.

Unfortunately, my husband was the poster child for this disease.

Some of the most intelligent and successful people in history have been diagnosed with this disorder, such as: Marilyn Monroe, Florence Nightingale, Edgar Allen Poe,

Frank Sinatra, Vincent Van Gogh, Robin Williams, Elvis Presley, Amy Winehouse, Kurt Cobain, Patty Duke and Emily Dickinson to name a few. (Note that a few of these people took their lives.)

As with many psychological issues there's both a physical and spiritual aspect of manic depression/bipolar disorder.

The term 'manic depressive' does not appear anywhere in the Bible, but the good book teaches us a lot of lessons we can apply to bipolar disorder.

Because B.D. (bipolar disorder) affects the way a person thinks, finding Godly counsel (Proverbs 1:5) and spending time in God's word (2 Timothy 3:16-17) are essential. Unfortunately John's and my walk was not with God—for if it was, things may have turned out different.

Up until that day I never knew what the term bi-polar or manic depressant meant, but it wasn't long that I became an expert on this subject for I bought and read every book that was written and asked doctors countless questions.

For the next several years my life turned upside down.

When John was manic he would spend money like there was no tomorrow. Luckily, he would make the money back by working twice as hard selling cars. One day he sold twenty cars on his own.

Although many people who are bi-polar can get violent in the manic stage John never laid a hand on me, but there were times I had to wedge a chair up against our bedroom door when we went to bed at night, so I could hear if he left the room. The reason for this was he told me when his ex-wife threatened to divorce him he went after her with a gun. When I questioned how he could do that he replied, "It wasn't loaded, I just wanted to scare her."

Because of his erratic behavior I found myself walking on eggshells, afraid he might snap at any moment.

My husband was Dr. Jekyll and Mr. Hyde--- a man whose moods swung like a pendulum.

Once the right medicine was given to him he was stabilized and our lives returned to somewhat normal. Through it all I grew closer to him for I now understood he had a sickness that made him act out. But this was just an excuse I convinced myself of.

******

After he was diagnosed I was forced on taking the role of a mother and a caretaker, instead of the lover and wife I had been in the beginning of our marriage.

Deep down I began resenting John for I hadn't signed up for this when I married him. I felt deceived and conned that I wed a man who wasn't the person I thought he was.

But I can't put all the blame on John for I was young and spoiled. I hadn't been that way before, but my husband doted on me so much it didn't take long to turn me into a spoiled brat.

This is something I'm not proud of. But although I was spoiled I wasn't selfish. In fact, I would literally take off my Rolex watch and give it to a family member if she wanted it. And my mother and son wanted for nothing. But like John, the more I got, the more I wanted.

Greed is a strong and selfish desire to have more of

something than is needed--most often money or power—and John and I both became very greedy.

There are many warnings in the Bible about giving in to greed and longing for riches.

Jesus warned, "*Watch out. Be on guard against all kinds of greed; a man's life does not consist in the abundance of his possessions.*" (Luke 12:15)

Money is a necessity and not a sin, but the love of money is.

"*For the love of money is a root of all kinds of evils. It is through this craving that some have wandered away from the faith and pierced themselves with many pangs.*" (Timothy 6:10)

******

Despite his periodical cycling we continued acquiring new business ventures and our success grew in leaps and bounds. One year we were voted "the most successful couple of the year" by the local banks.

We had all the money we could want or need, but it was never enough for John. This is a trait of a person who is bi-polar—they are never satisfied or happy with anything.

I know my husband loved me as much as he could love anyone, but in reality I was just the trophy--- the robotic Stepford wife who lost all identity in who she once was.

My life was now to please my husband and do anything to make and keep him happy. Although John gave me everything that money could buy, the one crucial thing missing was his respect.

******

On the onset of his cycling John began verbally abusing me. At times he would call me stupid and tell me that I was and never would be anything without him. He convinced me of this and soon I lost all my self-respect and self-worth.

I really believed I was the one with the problem.

It took me years to discover the truth, but I now realize it was John who had the problem. People like John are insecure and need to make others feel badly about themselves in order to feel adequate.

After our fights my husband would buy me a lavish piece of jewelry and tell me how sorry he was and would never do it again. But he did!

Looking back, I am furious at myself for not seeing what was happening. At that time I was a worn down woman who had a*llowed* her husband to rob her of her personal identity.

For years I blamed John-- that is, until the day I could look in the mirror and take full responsibility for my actions for you see I subconsciously allowed this behavior. But at that time I so desperately wanted that father figure to love me.

Unfortunately, it was always the *wrong* father I was seeking.

******

I guess the straw that broke the camels back was the time my husband wanted me to represent our state in a national beauty pageant.

It was a contest strictly for married women. John begged me to enter informing me it would be good for his business if I would compete, for he just *knew* I would win. After all, I was *his* wife so how could I lose?

Although I had experience as a model, I had zero in pageantry. There is a certain way beauty contestants walk and perform that signature wave. The way they smile and talk is something they are not born with but acquire through the training of a high paid coach.

Beauty pageantry has become a multi-million dollar business. It became part of the American society in the 1920's. The first known pageant was in 1839 when Georgiana Seymour, the Duchess of Somerset was crowned "The Queen of Beauty," which was held at the Eglinton Tournament.

The oldest pageant in the United States is Miss America, which was organized in 1921when founded by a local businessman as a means to entice tourists to Atlantic City, New Jersey.

Today there are hundreds of independent pageants such as Miss, Mrs., and Senior Miss, which attract women from all walks of life.

And then of course there are the controversial pageants for young children. Many mothers start their young daughters in these pageants, some as young as two years old.

Beauty pageants for children began in the 1960's and have become a huge industry in the U.S. Therapists admit that by putting your young child in one of these competitions makes them image obsessed, overly competitive and applies too much pressure on them.

Pageantry creates a negative and positive impact on young girls. Competing in pageants puts an unnecessary strain and emotional abuse on young children who are taught to behave like mini catwalk models—instead of playing with dolls and trucks.

Reluctantly, I granted John his wish, entering the local pageant and to my surprise I won. My husband was ecstatic and displayed a picture of me wearing the crown and sash in his office for everyone to see. He boasted there was no way I could lose the national for he would have never married anyone who wasn't a winner!

******

For the next several months I spent every waking minute practicing the walk and perfecting the wave, preparing for the national pageant. I was extremely stressed and under pressure, thus I lost ten pounds, which according to John was a blessing for I was a bit too chunky. (At that time I weighed 125 pounds)

The pageant would be televised live from Las Vegas. My entire family accompanied me for support. The seven days there with the other 52 contestants was an experience I will never forget for I befriended many wonderful women from all walks of life.

The age requirement was open wide: twenty-one through fifty years old.

Mrs. Washington, the winner, was twenty-one years old and had just married three months earlier, thus had no children. (She had a perfect body for there were no stretch marks)

When the pageant was over I walked away with the title of "Most Photogenic" and placed fifth. I couldn't wait to show off my trophies to John and my family.

While I was waiting back stage I noticed a few husbands bring flowers, telling their wives how proud of them they were.

One of the women was thrilled when her husband asked her to re-new their marriage vows.

Being the hopeless romantic I am, I thought this gesture was heart-warming and hoped John would do the same.

But when my husband came in I immediately noticed a look of disapproval on his face. He walked up to me and said, "I want a divorce. I'm embarrassed to go home with a loser!"

I stood there in disbelief as I watched the faces of the other contestants who heard what he said. My heart was broken as I stood there with my eyes swelling up.

I begged John not to leave me and apologized for not being pretty enough to win! Looking back I can't believe what a pathetic example of a woman I was!

******

After the pageant I returned home and remained with John for several more years. By then my son was in high school and I didn't want to take him away from his friends and the life he had made there. After all, he already went through one extremely painful time when I divorced his father.

It was about this time that I contacted a renowned psychic/medium named Sylvia after seeing her on a popular television show.

I had never been to a psychic and although I hadn't met Sylvia in person we connected instantly on the phone.

At that time I thought she really wanted to help for she felt sorry for me but now looking back I'm sure the heap of money I sent her had a lot to do with it.

Sylvia was no fly-by-night street corner psychic. She gained a worldwide reputation by assisting police authorities to locate missing people and her fame soared when she was on a television show and told the host that he had a debilitating disease, in which he knew nothing about at that time.

Every week I would call her and we would talk for one hour discussing my shaky marriage and emotionally abusive husband.

One day she asked a strange request. She wanted me to mail her something that belonged to my husband, saying she could draw his energy from it and be able to get a better feel of what was happening. The next day I sent Sylvia one of John's socks.

She called me the day she received it, counseling me to exit the marriage as soon as I could, stating my husband would ultimately kill me should I remain. She said John was a very sick man (mentally) and the abuse would soon turn from mental to physical.

That alarming statement lingered foremost in my mind and I found myself walking on eggshells not to upset him.

At that time I had no idea psychics were not Godly. I now know that astrologists, psychics, and channelers are dark. In Deuteronomy 18 it states, *"we are not to have anything to do with them."*

During those last years I remained with John there were good times and there were bad times. One day after one of our fights I got the courage to tell him I was unhappy and couldn't take it anymore. I told him I thought it would be better if we divorced. He flew into a rage and said he would kill me before he would let me go. His eyes were wild looking and he pushed me back into a wall.

That statement hit me like a ton of bricks affirming Sylvia's suspicions. Since my husband had been diagnosed bi-polar, I wasn't sure if he meant it but I wasn't about to wait around and find out. I also remembered that one time he had gone after his ex-wife with a gun to scare her-- although he told me it wasn't loaded.

As soon as my son graduated from high school, I gathered the courage to leave. I had been doing a lot of soul-searching and praying for God to show me the way. I fled in the middle of the day while John was at work, having it all planned out.

I left him a "Dear John" letter and drove south to Florida. Yes, it was the coward way but I was afraid for my life.

My mother, son and two dogs left with me as we set off to start a new life. I remember at the time feeling like a bird that had just been left out of his cage after years of being confined.

Looking back, I should have sat down with John face to face, but I was scared of him and thought he would talk me into staying, which I probably would have.

I know we are not supposed to look back, but I still do and regret that day.

Although I divorced John, I remained good friends with him up until his death for I have always been the type of person who looks at the good in people and tends to forget the bad.

John had a lot of good in him-- he was just a mentally sick, insecure man who was totally lost in the darkness.

Ten years after our divorce John got very sick and called asking if I would fly there. Without hesitation, I bought an airline ticket and flew up north.

I'm so glad I did for it gave me the opportunity to tell him how much I loved him and forgave him for the things he did.

That was the final closure we both needed. I made the peace I had to make with him and myself.

When I arrived at the hospital I was shocked to see the man I once idolized. The strong and handsome man was now thin, depressed and sad.

Although he couldn't talk well because of the stroke, he mumbled asking why I waited so long to visit. He asked me to stroll him in the wheelchair to get some fresh air.

I wrapped a blanket around him and took him outside so he could hear the birds and feel the April sun.

When we went back inside I crawled into his hospital bed and read psalms and scriptures from the Bible. He listened as tears rolled down his face. I kissed him goodbye and told him I'd be back the next day.

The next morning I got a call that John died in the night.

It's really ironic for he always said his one wish was to die in my arms. I guess his wish came true.

I know I was supposed to be there with him for before he passed I read him the Word. I have no doubt that someday we will once again be together—but this time it will be in total love and peace.

Isaiah 55:6-7 *"Seek the Lord while he may be found; call upon Him while He is near; let the wicked forsake his ways, and the unrighteous thoughts. Let him return to the Lord, that he may have compassion on him, and to our God, for he will abundantly pardon."*

5 Free At Last

After my divorce I made plans to move to South Florida and start my new life with a clean slate. My son would be attending college there, so I wouldn't be too far away from him.

Since most of our conjugal worth was acquired during our marriage I was entitled to one-half of our assets.

During the divorce proceeding, the judge asked why I was only seeking a small portion of the money, being entitled to fifty percent. I stated I didn't want to hurt John's business and what I was receiving would be adequate. In addition, I testified my husband's murder threat were I to leave and take any money.

The judge lectured my husband imploring, "You can't do that!" to which he replied, "It was merely an idle threat intending to scare her into not leaving."

John got up from his chair and said, "I just lost the best thing that ever happened to me," as he left the room with tears in his eyes.

******

When I moved to Florida I felt like an eighteen-year-old girl just beginning her life. I didn't look like a woman in her forties and certainly didn't act like one.

Since I had spent the last twenty some years with only two men (my husbands) I never had time to sow any wild oats.

I contacted a real estate agent and bought a mini-mansion in a ritzy part of town, for I was accustomed to this lavish lifestyle, which I felt both entitled to and deserving of.

I can see God chuckling for all of these things we call ours-- material or otherwise—belong to Him. He just lets us borrow them for a little while, but can remove them as quickly as He donates them----as I personally found out.

After my divorce I stayed in contact with Sylvia who informed me the home I just bought was originally constructed over Indian burial ground. How she knew that I don't know, but at the time I didn't take her seriously.

It didn't take me long to get right into the swing of things of a single life. I became a regular at the local clubs and discos and being the "new girl in town" I was in demand.

Naturally I loved all this new attention and as my girlfriends did I sampled a different flavor (of man) every month.

Occasionally, I even juggled two different men--- dating one in the afternoon and the second at night. I wasn't what you would call a 'loose goose,' but I certainly did my share of flirting and teasing.

Eventually I met Bob, a guy who sold yachts to the rich and famous and knew a lot of high rollers. We started dating and seemed to hit it off.

I accompanied Bob to the Caribbean island of St.

Maarten where his best friend, the owner of a gigantic cosmetic company moored his mega million 524-foot luxury yacht--large enough to accommodate his personal helicopter.

I met the owner and his trophy girlfriend who was decades younger and the four of us sailed the Caribbean. (Of course the girlfriend was his mistress as there was a wife and children living back in Europe.)

On the last night of our trip the four of us overindulged in several bottles of pink champagne. Being a lightweight in the liquor department, I passed out on a couch. A short time later I awoke looking for my date.

I stumbled into one of the bedrooms and saw Bob in bed with the owner's girl. Embarrassed and shocked I quietly left the room.

As I was walking down the hall I noticed the owner exiting another bedroom. As he passed me I saw a female employee lying on his bed, totally naked. That was my first encounter into the world of bed hopping, that many of the beautiful people indulge in to keep amused.

I never confronted Bob about what I saw. When we returned home I thanked him for the trip and said I thought it was better we didn't see each other anymore.

I think he knew why.

******

After the incident on the yacht I decided to take a sabbatical from dating and hang with the girls. It was safer that way and a lot less heartache.

One night my girlfriends and I went to dinner at a

swanky Miami restaurant and had left my phone in the car. I walked outside to where my car was parked and passed the valet who was now sitting in a car across from mine.

It was October 31—Halloween--- and the streets were full of costumed revelers, partying and looking ghoulish.

I've always liked the holiday for I got to dress up and fantasize of being someone else for a night.

Some Christians look at Halloween as a pagan holiday where the devil is worshipped and evil is glorified. Many churches have replaced Halloween with Fall Festivals that are more family-friendly and allow a safer environment and fun alternative to trick-or-treating.

As I was walking to my car I heard someone say, "You're not leaving already, are you?"

To my surprise it was my waiter who went to the car the valet was sitting in. I noticed the attendant was talking on a cell phone and looking across at me.

Call it woman's intuition or a gut feeling, I felt uneasy so I stayed in my car for about 10 minutes. When the waiter got out he returned to the restaurant and the valet went back to his station. I retrieved my phone and got out of my car.

As I was locking the door a voice said, "Give me your jewelry." I turned and saw a young man wearing a devil's mask. I laughed and brushed it off as a Halloween prank.

He pulled out a shiny blade and held it to me chest. Again he stuttered, "Give me your jewelry," as he added pressure to the blade.

In that moment my entire life flashed before me.

It happened so quickly but seemed like an eternity.

The masked robber removed my Rolex watch from my wrist and my ex-husbands diamond ring that I still wore. As he pushed me to the ground, the mask fell off. I screamed for help as he fled into the street allowing me to briefly see his face.

By this time my girlfriend was worried why I hadn't come back after 10 minutes and came looking for me. As she was walking past the valet she heard me calling out and ran to me.

The valet was oblivious, saying he heard and seen nothing.

Within minutes the police arrived and questioned everyone in the vicinity, but since no one saw anything no arrests were made and my jewelry was never found.

For years I was angry and upset that my jewelry was stolen. After all these jewels belonged to *me!*

I now know they were just *things* that I *though*t I needed to make me happy.

******

I've always been a very outgoing girl who made friends easily.

Within a matter of weeks moving to Florida, I had a new group of friends, including a man named Kurt who was an acclaimed attorney.

I first met Kurt when I was seeking a lawyer to look over my property settlement to give me a second opinion-- even though my divorce was finalized. Kurt came highly recommended as a man of integrity.

We quickly became good friends.

Up until that time I didn't do much traveling due to the fact that my husband John never wanted to leave his business. (And the one thing I loved to do was travel.)

Several months after my divorce I booked a two-week African safari. I went to the doctor to get several immunizations that were required to leave the country.

Two days later I became deathly ill. It appeared I was allergic to one of the shots and had to be hospitalized. Sadly, I canceled my African trip.

Three weeks after getting out of the hospital, Kurt called and asked if I would like to accompany him to Australia on a *spiritual* trip. He said we would be traveling the country and the itinerary included visiting an Aboriginal tribe.

Kurt's fiancée, a top surgeon, couldn't make it due to her heavy workload and he didn't want to cancel. Having missed my African trip I jumped at the chance to go, but Kurt warned me "this would be a trip like none I had ever experienced before and my life would never be the same."

Apparently, the woman in charge named Dr. J. was a noted channeler —whatever that meant. I knew nothing of channelers and spiritual journeys, but I would soon find out.

I was still in touch with the psychic, Sylvia, so I called and told her about this spiritual journey and asked if she had heard about Dr. J.

She told me she was aware of the channeler, and saw

no harm in my going to Australia for it was one of the most spiritual places on Earth and spending time with an Aboriginal tribe was a once in a lifetime opportunity.

When I hung up, I called Kurt and booked the trip.

Leviticus 19:31 *"Do not turn to mediums or seek out spiritists, for you will be defiled by them."*

6   Going Down Under

I had heard about spirituality but never understood it's meaning, nor was I familiar with the term channeler.

Channelers, sometimes referred to as channels arc psychic mediums that focus on communicating with spirit guides, ascended masters, and angels.

A channeler conveys thoughts or energy from a source believed to be outside the person's body or conscious mind.

Traditionally channelers are channeling messages from advanced spirits--- usually to communicate spiritual wisdom about life and the afterlife.

Dr. J was an author and professor at a well-known western university. She channeled a spirit named Kathumi who is said to have served with Jesus as a teacher and is a reincarnation of Pythagoras—the Greek philosopher and mathematician.

It is written that Kathumi was also the reincarnation of Balthazar—one of the three magi (wise men from the East who paid homage to baby Jesus, and the co-protector of the Holy Grail—the ancient quest for self awareness.)

This 'master' was the doorkeeper of ancient occult mysteries and I knew that anything related to black magic, astrology, or the supernatural, so of course I was skeptical of Dr. J and her association with this so called spirit, Kathumi.

When I got off the plane in Sydney, Dr. J walked up to me and said, "We have been waiting for you, Victoria. You make the 50th person," which meant nothing to me at the time.

The other forty-nine people in the group consisted of doctors, lawyers, healers, and teachers. Most had been on one of these spiritual trips before and several had even accompanied Dr. J on one of her journeys.

The very first night our group was invited to a pig roast held at a farm. The weather was perfect and the sky was illuminated with thousands of stars.

This particular group consisted of forty-five women and five men. One of the men named Michael was a New York Stockbroker with Wall Street connections. As soon as we met, Michael and I clicked--not so much physically, but felt like we had known each other for years.

When the pig roast was over our group returned to the hotel. We had been coupled in rooms and my roommate was a quiet woman named Sara.

After we got back to the hotel several people said they were not tired and wanted to hang out awhile. Sara, Michael, myself, and two other women sat by the pool admiring the perfect weather.

One by one the others excused themselves saying they were tired and going to bed, leaving only Michael and I.

I looked at my watch. It read 3 AM—what the spiritual world refers to as "the power hour." It is between the hours of three and four when extraordinary occurrences can and do occur.

3 AM is also known as the "demons hour," because it's exactly 12 hours after the hour Jesus died. (3 PM)

This is the hour the sky is at its darkest and darkness is power to demons. Many occultists, paranormal experts, voodoo practitioners and doers of black magic admit that 3 AM is when their spells have maximum power.

There have been Christians that have come forth stating they experienced great spiritual trials and tribulations that occurred during this hour.

In Christianity the number 3 means divine perfection. Christians know that the number 3 is the number of the trinity, the Godhead--- consisting of God the Father, the Son, and God the Holy Spirit, which indicates wholeness and an inner sanctity.

The number 3 is extremely significant and can be seen hundreds of times in the Bible. Such as, *Noah had three sons* (Gen 6:10), *Job had three daughters* (Job 1:2), *the Ark of the Covenant contained three sacred objects*, (Heb. 9:4), and most important *Jesus Christ arose on the third day.* (1 Corinthians 15)

Also, Jesus resuscitates a dead body three times in the Bible and sadly fell three times when carrying the cross.

Of the 12 Apostles, it is written that Jesus loved 3 of them more than the rest. They are Peter and brothers John and James and were allowed to witness his Transfiguration, another example of 3, when he suddenly stood talking in bright white clothing with Moses and Elijah.

And it is on the third day of creation that Earth was made; the placard on the cross is written in 3 languages, and Satan tempts Jesus 3 times before giving up.*

******

Only minutes before I looked at my watch, the sky was brightly lit with stars painted from one side to the other; but in a matter of seconds it turned its darkest ebony. Suddenly, there were no stars or chirping crickets and all went silent.

I looked at Michael and asked, "What's going on?" which he replied, "I don't know, but something's definitely wrong."

I felt like I was in an episode of The Twilight Zone as a shooting meteorite streaked across the ebony, starless sky. As we both watched Michael and I said in unison, "Wow! Did you see that?"

Instantly the sky was lit as bright as it had been before. I glanced at my watch that now read 3:25 AM. Where did 25 minutes go?

Looking at the sky I asked, "Do you see those stars over there? Not the thousand scattered across the sky…. but those stars over *there*. It's like they're angels and I'm dancing with them," I said to Michael.

He looked at me as if I were crazy, but politely answered, "Yea, right."

******

The next morning when our group boarded the bus we explained what Michael and I had experienced the night before. We told Dr. J about the loss of 25 minutes and the shooting star.

She went to her briefcase and retrieved a transcript she had typed three months earlier while channeling Kathumi. It read, "Under the star lit sky in February, a woman and man would be chosen to lead the group opening the portals between Heaven and earth." Dr. J said, "Victoria and Michael are the chosen ones."

Everyone got quiet. I sat there in disbelief and wondered how this letter dated three months earlier, depicted exactly what happened to us the night before.

After several minutes of silence, Michael told Dr. J about the Angels I *thought* I saw when I pointed to certain stars.

She laughed and brought out a painting illustrating a sky lit with hundreds of stars and a shooting meteorite.

I stammered, "There's my stars!" and pointed to the section of stars I saw the night before.

Dr. J replied, "Michael was stopped, but Victoria was brought into the fifth dimension!"

"The fifth dimension! What the heck is that? The only fifth dimension I know is the singing group," I said.

She explained that dimensions are states of consciousness available to anyone who vibrates in resonance with the specific frequencies and opportunities available within each dimension.

Dr. J told us planet earth is located in the third dimension. The transition from the third dimension consciousness to fourth dimension consciousness is a protolotype of Earth's future and is also an energy gateway through which humans pass during death and rebirth. When a person reaches fifth dimension consciousness their perception of time may slow down considerably.

She continued by saying that a person who has reached the fifth dimension consciousness may also experience increased psychic and intuitive abilities, such as clairvoyance, claircognizance, telepathy, premonitions, ESP and psychometry.

Human beings have a 3 dimensional reality: length, width and breadth. Some scientists say the fifth dimension exists outside a humans' ability to see it because it is so small, it's like trying to see an ant atop a garden hose.

The fifth dimension is the spiritual realm---a place you cannot find with a telescope, nor is it simply 'invisible' to our naked eye for our eyes can't see the infrared or ultraviolet frequencies where the spiritual realm lies.

Everyone on the bus was completely captivated at what our hostess told us. Just when I thought I heard it all she counseled, "It is in the fifth dimension where Arcturus is-- one of the most advanced extraterrestrial civilizations in our galaxy and where the extraterrestrials called Pleiadians live."

It was this time when I started questioning if I had been drugged or perhaps a spell was put on me?

******

What does the Bible say about other dimensions?

Although the Bible is not a science textbook, it is accurate in what it does portray about world and universe.

The Bible says that for God "a thousand years in your sight are like a day that has just gone by." Psalm 90:4

But throughout the readings in the Bible there are many passages in the holy book that can be interpreted to prove the existence of higher dimensions.

Isaiah 8:19 And when they say to you, "inquire of the mediums and the true necromancers who chirp and mutter, Should not a people inquire of their God? Should they inquire of the dead on behalf of the living?"

7   An Alien Abduction or a Bad Dream?

I've always been fascinated by the unknown.

There was a time as a teenager when I was very sick with a high fever. As I was lying in bed I saw an angel with open wings hover over me. I screamed for my mother who of course saw nothing.

Was I hallucinating from the fever?

Another time walking home from school I saw my grandmother coming towards me on the sidewalk smiling.

I ran home hysterical for my grandmother had died a few years earlier.

I was always naïve. There was a time when I attended a magic show in Las Vegas with my husband, John. The magician told the entire audience of about 150 people to touch their noses.

After we did he said to remove our fingers, which everyone could but me. I tried to move them but it felt like my fingers were glued to my nose.

John got upset thinking I was playing along. He told me to quit fooling around, but even after he tried to pry my finger it would not budge. The magician assured the audience I would be able to remove them in an hour, which I did.

******

Is it the human mind that is so very suggestive or do incomprehensible things happen to certain people?

Some believe you can create anything by allowing the mind to do what it was created by God to do. The human mind is very powerful and unlimited in potential. It is said that the mind has the power to heal all diseases.

There are many theories about the human mind. Some ancient civilizations refer to it as the connection between the body and the soul.

The mind is a set of cognitive faculties, including consciousness, perception, thinking, judgment, language and memory.

In the average person only 10% of brain capacity is actually utilized. Imagine what we could accomplish using the full capacity.

******

The following events you are about to read really DID happen. I give you my word there were no drugs, no alcohol and no hypnotizing-----that I am cognizant of.

After the incident in Australia the group started calling me "the virgin child." That was really funny because I was not a virgin and certainly not a child. The reason for naming me that was I was "completely pure" in the sense of spirituality.

After my experience with the meteorite many unexplainable things began happening.

One day after sightseeing when we returned to our hotel every time I would turn the light on in my room it would flicker as if it were a Morse code.

I summoned Dr. J who counseled, "They are trying to contact me."

I asked her who 'they' were and she responded, "the other night when you lost time you were abducted by the alien species called Pleiadians. They are trying to make contact with you."

Mortified I asked, "What did they do to me? What do they want?"

Dr. J reassured me they didn't and wouldn't harm me and she was monitoring their actions. She said the Pleiadians were the nicest of all alien species.*

Abduction, the loss of time, the Pleiadians---I began questioning what was happening. Was it demonic and evil?

I sought my friend Kurt who was a straight shooter and respected attorney asking what he thought was happening.

Surprisingly, he didn't seem at all concerned. He said the reason I had been selected was because I chose the spiritual path rather than the material by leaving the riches I once possessed with my ex-husband.

For the next week our group visited different cities throughout Australia, including Perth, which is the most populous city and capital of western Australia. For several days, nothing out of the ordinary occurred. Just when I started to feel at ease what happened next still seems inconceivable.

Psalm 144:11 *"Deliver me; rescue me from the hands of foreigners whose mouths are full of lies, whose right hands are deceitful."*

*rational wiki.org
* Pleiadians are said to lack pigmentation in their skin and hair, giving them an albino appearance. Many have an Asian appearance similar to the species known as 'grays.'

8 ⟩ The Olgas

Our next stop was to visit the Olgas--a group of thirty-six large domed rock formations located about 227 miles south west of Alice Spring.

They are the oldest known geologic formation that has its genesis in mythology as being the center of the Aboriginals world.

According to the Aboriginal legends, during the mythtic period in the beginning of the world known as Alcheringa, (the Dreamtime) ancestral beings in the form of totemic animals and humans emerged from the interior of the Australian soil. *

As these Dreamtime ancestors roamed the Earth they created features of the landscape through everyday action such as birth, play, singing, fishing, hunting marriage and death.

At the end of the Dreamtime these creatures turned into stone and the bodies of the ancestors turned into hills, caves, lakes and other landforms, making places such as Ayers Rock and the Olgas sacred sites.

By Aboriginal tradition only certain elderly males are permitted to climb the rock, but despite the tradition the Australian government allows tourists to make the climb.

At one time there used to be 12 different walks around

the Olga's, but only 2 remain today. The other 10 have been closed to protect the fragile environment, but mostly to allow the Aboriginal owners of the land to conduct their ancient ceremonies in privacy. The area is closed not only to white people but also off limits to other Aboriginals not native to that specific area.

When we arrived at the Olgas, as the others exited the bus, I froze unable to move. I didn't know why until a woman in our group said, "Its ok, I was there with you."

Michael saw the expression on my face and came over to see what was wrong. I told him I envisioned myself as a Native American girl in a past life being sacrificed and thrown off the Olga!

Why did I say that?

The woman sitting behind me said she was also sacrificed in a past life with me.

But she told me that *before* I told them what I saw.

Shaking, I walked over to our group who had now split into two, forming large circles while holding hands and meditating and praying. I walked over and joined in.

Dr. J appointed one person to stand in the middle of the circle, meditating on each person's third eye.

After a few minutes Tom, the man who was in the middle of our circle stopped praying and summoned Dr. J.

They called me over to the side and informed me when Tom got to me he saw a brilliant white light. He said he had never experienced anything like that before.

I asked Dr. J what this all meant. She said, "It was a good thing because anything to do with 'the light' is from God".

As our group and other tourists were busy photographing the beautiful, orange mounds, I robotically sauntered to the entrance of the one Olga and walked inside.

Michael was on my left and Cherie, a healer from New York was on my right. At that time we were unaware that entering the cave was prohibited.

Kurt appeared and yelled, "Hey you can't go in there. These are forbidden grounds," to which I replied, "You are supposed to be here, too."

Methodically, two women from our group joined us inside the cave. That made six of us: Cherie, Michael, Kurt, me, and the two women named Mary and Angel.

Once inside we took our positions and didn't utter a word ---we just joined hands and prayed.

I was later told the next thing that happened was I broke away from the circle and fell to the ground. Several minutes later I rose and said, "Its not over yet," and laid back on the hard ground.

When I rose the second time I felt like I was 200 years old. I had no energy and couldn't walk, so the others literally carried me back to the bus. When we arrived Dr. J was very upset that we were not there at the designated time.

One by one they told her what they had experienced. They said they saw me enter the Olga and like a piece of metal drawn to a magnet, they followed.

After we started to pray and I fell to the ground they

heard loud cries and moans coming from underneath and inside the cave walls.

Then they said Kurt began chanting in a foreign language.

Right before I rose the second time my five friends observed thousands of light beams emanate from the ground, shoot up through my body and into the ceilings of the cave.

Dr. J didn't seem surprised explaining, "the six of us acted as a hexagram and together were conduits releasing thousands of Aboriginal souls that had been trapped for centuries."

At the time I didn't know what a hexagram was but later discovered its a six-pointed star that has long been used in magic, occultism, witchcraft and astrology. The symbol is comprised of a six within a six within a six, which is 666--- the number of the beast. *

I knew that the number of the Beast, 666, is associated with the mark of the Beast and the name of the Beast (the antichrist) and is described in the book of Revelation. *

Our entire bus remained silent during the ride back home.

When I got to my hotel room I fell into a deep coma-like sleep.

* The first beast comes "out of the sea" and is given authority and power by the dragon. The second beast comes from "out of the earth" and directs all peoples of the earth to worship the first beast.

Revelation 13:17 *"And that no man might buy or sell, save he that had the mark, or the name of the beast, or the number of his name."*

*Wikipedia

9 ⟩ Living with the Aboriginals

After the Olga incident I wasn't sure what was real and what wasn't. But since five intelligent people experienced the same thing—I came to the conclusion that it really did happen.

Our next stop was visiting an Aboriginal tribe who lived in the bush. I was really excited about going to meet and learn about these people for their lifestyle intrigued me.

There are about 500 different Aboriginal tribes residing in Australia, each with their own language and territory; most who live in the outback.

Archaeologists believe that the Aboriginals first settled in Australia around 40,000 years ago, originally emanating from Africa through India and the East Indies.

Their history is both interesting and sad. Ever since the British conquered Australia, Aboriginals have had their land confiscated-- similar to the American Indians.

During the 20th century the Aboriginal extermination was replaced by a policy of extracting the children from their parents--- either placing them with white families or in mission schools.

The purpose was to eradicate traces of Aboriginal culture and language. Today, these people still face racist attitudes and occasionally there are incidents of violence towards them.

The generally poor living conditions cause Aboriginal people to have a far higher infant mortality and suicide rate, and a lower life expectancy than the rest of Australia's population.

Aboriginals are said to be the most spiritual people in the world for they are preoccupied with the connection of the earth, nature, and people. They are very religious people but rather than praying to a single God they cannot see, each group believes in a number of different deities.

There is not one deity covering all of Australia. Each tribe has its own with an overlap of beliefs just as there is an overlap of words between language groups.

Aboriginal deities have many roles and no single description or term that can describe all of them. Based on their primary role they fall into three main categories. Any one deity may belong to one, two, or all three of these categories: (a) Creation Beings, (b) Ancestral Beings and (c) Totemic Beings.

The Creation Beings are involved with the creation of people, the landscape and aspects of the environment.

The Ancestral Beings are regarded as the direct ancestors of the people living today and the Totemic Beings represent the original form of an animal, plant, or other object.

******

When we arrived at the bush a female translator named Anna, an American woman in her forties approached us. You could tell she lived and breathed this life for she was dressed in ragged, dirty clothes; but was as sweet as could be and accommodating to us all.

As we were walking Anna commented on my earrings.

They were expensive costume jewelry made of sterling silver called 'Lunch at the Ritz.' I thanked her and we continued our tour.

When she introduced us to the tribal chief I was taken back.

He was a very old man with a white beard and shoulder length curly hair.

His skin was dark-- darker than an African-- and he had a flat, broad nose. His chest was bare and he sported a red scarf that covered his private area.

On his body were brightly painted patterns. Anna explained the designs reflect the persons relationship and standing (ranks) in the community.

The most distinctive trait of an Aboriginal is their piercing eyes for they are very dark—almost black, and appear to be imbedded deeply.

In their native language the Chief talked to Anna who interpreted everything to us—mostly describing their lives and traditions.

Once again Anna commented on my earrings.

Without thinking I removed and gave them to her.

She seemed surprised and thanked me saying she had no use for them, living in the bush. I told her to take them for she liked them more than I needed them.

The others asked why I would give away a piece of

jewelry that was obviously expensive. I replied, "They are just material things."

After I handed Anna the earrings she told the Chief what I had done and he asked me to remove my sunglasses. When I took them off the Chief looked into my eyes and replied I was a very old soul. He said he would like me to stay with his family as their special guest in the bush.

At first I didn't know what to say, but Dr. J stated what an honor this was and that I should stay with them.

Being the girly girl I am I said, "I can't stay. I don't have my make-up or clothes."

Anna laughed and said I wouldn't need them!

I agreed to stay with the Chief and his clan until my group returned for me three days hence. Those next several days were some of the most amazing and happiest days of my life.

******

The tribe consisted of 15 Aboriginals: four women, four men and seven children. At night I slept alongside the children on the hard ground under a man made tent.

Our meals consisted of fish and rabbit that they killed with a bow and arrow. There was an abundance of berries, figs and wild plums that were constantly being offered to me. Some of the children munched on turtles and ducks, which I politely refused.

Their life was very simple. The children amused themselves by playing the traditional Aboriginal games that are inclusive and non-competitive.

During the day the women painted on canvas they sold

in the village, (I was given a painting of The Seven Sisters that is hanging in my home) while the men went hunting food.

Anna explained that the Star Dreaming story of the Seven Sisters is one of the oldest stories amongst the Aboriginals.

The story relates to the journey of the seven sisters that make up the star cluster known as the Pleiades (* note: you will be reading about this star cluster throughout)

In the Seven Sisters story the group of stars are Napaljarri sisters from one skin group. The sisters are often expressed carrying the Jampijinpa man Wardilyka, who is in love with the women.

Then the morning star, Jukurra-jukurra, who is a Jakamarra man and who is also in love with the seven Napaljarri sisters, is known chasing them across the night sky. They are seen to be running away, fleeing from the man who wants to take one of the sisters for his wife. However, under traditional law, the man pursuing the sisters is the wrong skin group and is forbidden to take a Napaljarri wife.

So the Seven Sisters are running away from the Jampijinpa man, they travel across the land and then from a steep hill they launch themselves into the sky in an attempt to escape.

******

The Aboriginal women were primarily topless and wore material that covered their private parts, as did the men. Though there was no verbal communication between the Aboriginals and myself, somehow we understood one another's needs.

They were just as inquisitive about me as I was with

them; especially the children who liked to run their fingers through my light colored hair and feel my facial features.

Three days later Dr. J and the group returned for me.

I didn't want to leave for I had never felt so tranquil and content. This new simple way of life seemed to agree with me far better than the hectic material world I had been living in.

As I was saying my sad good-byes to my new family the chief told Anna there was something very important I had to do in this lifetime. When I asked what it was he answered, "I would know."

****

When I got back home, my mother noticed a drastic change in me stating she never saw me so content and peaceful. I think that experience of living with the Aboriginals confirmed that material things were not the answer to true happiness.

The Aboriginals are indigenous whose lifestyle is as simple as can be and said to be the happiest people on the planet for they discovered that true happiness comes from within.

After staying with them I couldn't agree more. I will be forever grateful that I had the opportunity to spent three days with some of the most righteous people ever created.

Proverb 16 *"Better is a little with the fear of the Lord, than with great treasure with trouble."*

10 ⟩ Oscar: An Uninvited Guest

When I returned to the States my friends were anxious to hear about my trip down under. I was apprehensive as to how how they would react when hearing my bizarre events. I knew I shouldn't care what they thought, but I have always been sensitive to criticism.

After all if someone had told me the story I was about to tell I would probably think they were delusional and psychotic.

I did tell my mother who immediately took me to to Church and had our Priest bless my house and me. The events didn't really surprise her for she always said, "Bizarre and crazy things always happened to me."

But I suspected after she heard what occurred in Australia, perhaps she thought I might have been drugged without my knowledge. (Like when Jim Jones, the religious leader and founder of the Peoples Temple in Jonestown, Guyana, murdered 909 of his members by giving them a cyanide poison to drink.)

✱✱✱✱✱✱

Before my Australian trip, I had been dating a man named George. A few days after I returned home, he came to see me.

At first I didn't tell him of my experiences for I wasn't ready to be questioned and interrogated.

One day he went to the kitchen for a drink of water and heard the muffled sound of a man clearing his throat, but when he turned around there was nobody there. George ran upstairs looking like he saw a ghost and told me what he heard but I brushed it off---that is, until that night after he left and I was taking a bath.

Baths have always been one of my favorite pleasures in life and the tub in my house was an oversized Jacuzzi. After George left I was relaxing in total serenity with the jets on, candles lit, and listening to the sound of Enigma—a group noted for soft, spiritual music.

Suddenly I saw visions dressed in long, dark robes in my bedroom, which is adjacent to the bathroom. I immediately jumped out of the tub and covered myself with a towel.

I called mom and a girlfriend describing what happened, insisting they come over and spend the night for I was now afraid to be there alone. They came right over, calmed me down and told me I probably had jet lag from the long trip back and was just over tired.

Shortly later we retired to separate bedrooms.

It was 3 AM (note that hour again) when I heard a blood-curdling scream come from the downstairs bedroom. Mom and I ran downstairs and found my girlfriend crying and shaking, swearing she felt *someone* or *something* rub up against her in the bed.

Shaken, the three of us slept together in my bed -- although I don't think any of us really slept.

******

All was quiet for the next few weeks.

Just when I was beginning to forget the incident my friend had, a second bizarre incident occurred.

George and I had an argument and we decided to break it off completely once and for all. I was feeling pretty lousy for my record in choosing men was shoddy.

It was mid afternoon and I decided to go upstairs and take a nap. It was a bright and sunny day, so I drew my blinds to darken the room. Before long I fell into a deep asleep.

A short time later I heard a loud thud like something hitting my window. I jumped up and pulled back the blinds, but saw nothing out of place so I went back to bed and fell asleep. When I awoke several hours later and went to the bathroom I noticed an antique lamp lying on the bottom of the bathtub.

At first I thought I was dreaming for the fixture was something I didn't own. I was positive that I didn't own this and had ever seen it before in my life.

It couldn't have gotten there by anyone else for nobody had a key to my house.

Perplexed and frightened I ran to the phone and called my friend, Kurt, who I hadn't seen since the Australia trip. I knew that nothing I told him would raise his eyebrows, for he also participated in the Olga experience.

When Kurt came over and saw the lamp he suggested we call a woman he knew in North Carolina. He said her name was Jane and she was known for cleansing unwanted spirits.

We called Jane and explained to her about the light and she agreed to fly in the next week.

When I hung up I phoned a realtor and listed my house on the market.

Matthew 12:43 *"Now when the unclean spirit goes out of the man, it passes through waterless places seeking rest, and does not find it."*

11 Sending Oscar Back

After that night my girlfriend felt something rubbing against her, I'd ask several friends to spend the night with me. I was scared to undress, take a bath, and be alone in my own house.

On occasion one of my friends would hear the muffled sound of a throat clearing like Michael had, but when they investigated there was nobody there.

I remembered what Sylvia the psychic told me about my house being built on top of an Indian burial ground.

Could this be significant? Were there angry Indian spirits who wanted me out of my house?

Needless to say my imagination was now running wild. I remembered watching the movie Poltergeist and how a contractor built homes over graves, causing unrest among the dead.

My house was located near the water in a luxury development and listed well below market value. Though potential buyers seemed to love everything about it, especially the low price, it didn't sell. In fact, I didn't even get an offer that I could counter-offer because if I had no matter how low it was I probably would have accepted it.

The feedback from the real estate agent was always the same.

She said the buyers loved everything about it but said it just wasn't the right house for them.

*****

I counted the days until Jane's visit. When she arrived at my house, as she walked through my front door she stopped, gasped for air and placed her hand over her heart. At first I wasn't sure if she was having an asthma or heart attack.

Jane told Kurt and I when entering my home the energy was overbearing. As she walked upstairs to my bedroom and bathroom where the supernatural events took place she laughed saying, "My bedroom was a spiritual playground."

When I asked what she meant Jane said, "There were many, many spirits there from the light, except for one. * This particular spirit was a disgruntled male who had grown very attached to me."

Jane said I unknowingly brought this spirit back to the States from Australia. The mere thought of an unknown being in my house who was obsessed with me was terrifying.

I then showed Jane the peculiar antique light that mysteriously appeared in my tub. After looking it over she explained, "I was a light worker and the antique light was a sign confirming this."

"What is a light worker and what does this spirit want from me?" I asked.

She explained that light workers are God's people with

global missions in life to make a positive difference in our failing world.

Light workers are those who volunteered before birth to help the planet and its' population heal from the effects of fear.

I recalled the Aboriginal Chief's message that I had something very important to do in my life. Could this be what he meant?

Jane explained light workers feel compelled to take on global missions that involved helping people, animals, and the environment, or a good cause other than themselves.

They are super sensitive to other people's needs, which may not always be a good thing as the light worker absorbs energies from other's moods.

Light workers in essence are caretakers radiating healing energy that soothes others. This is because they truly care about people and wish that everyone could be happy, healthy and provided for.

Wow! This certainly sounded like me, as I've always been one who went out of her way to particularly help animals.

Actually, I'm an exceptionally sensitive person who has always been a caretaker--- often to a deleterious degree--- and by being the "mama bear" to many people, I have gotten offended and dumped on many times.

I asked Jane how to rid this so-called spirit that was not from the light. Her answer had me doubting her mental health and authenticity. *

She told me I had to lie on the floor in a fetal position, give this spirit a name and demand that it goes back where it came from.

When she said this Kurt and I looked at one another in disbelief, but at that point I was willing to do just about anything to expel whatever "it" was.

As I positioned myself on the floor Jane warned me that whatever happened---I could NOT touch it. I looked at her like she was crazy for the last thing I wanted to do was touch it.

I curled in a fetal position and yelled, "Oscar, go back where you came from."

(Don't ask me where I got that, but it was the first name that came out of my mouth.)

While demanding the spirit to return to his place of origin, I felt a strange swooshing sensation coming from of my lower back.

It felt like a vacuum sucking something out of me.

Not realizing what I was doing, I reached out my arms to grab whatever "it" was. When Jane saw what I was doing she warned me not to touch it.

The next thing I knew I felt like myself again. The only way to explain it was when I had given birth to my son Joey the labor pains were in my lower back, not in the front. That is exactly how it felt when Oscar evacuated my body.

Early the next morning I got a phone call from the realtor telling me that a couple accepted the asking price and the house was sold! I had one month to vacate what had become a house of horrors.

* The Bible clearly rules that man lives once on this earth before eternity. After judgment God teaches us not to give to anyone total control of our mind and He wants us to be conscience, with a healthy mind and proper will to choose to be obedient to Him.

James 4:7 *"Submit yourselves, therefore to God. Resist the devil and he will flee from you."*

Genesis 3:14 *And the Lord God said," unto the serpent, because thou has done this, thou are cursed above all cattle and about every beast of the field: upon thy belly shalt thou go and dust shall thou eat all the days of thy life."*

* In the Bible it says there are 2 types of spirit beings-- the unfallen holy angels and the angels that followed Satan in his rebellion. The only time the Bible talks of demons being transferred from one creature to another was when Jesus transferred the legion of demons from possessed men into a herd of pigs. Matthew 8:28

12 ▸ Hyptnosis and Regression

(What you are about to read may be hard to believe but the events occurred and have been verified and documented by notable professionals.)

After I moved out of my house I still had a hard time relaxing due to the strange experiences I had lived through the past year. I had trouble sleeping at night and jumped at the slightest sound.

I called Sylvia who recommended I see a hypnosis/hypnotherapy specialist in Miami. She said he was among the leading doctors in the United States who specialized in transgression, of which I knew nothing about.

Sylvia explained that past life regression is a technique that uses hypnosis to recover what practitioners believe is memories of past lives or incarnations. P.L.R. (past life regression) is typically undertaken either in pursuit of a spiritual experience or in a psychotherapeutic setting.

Growing up Catholic I was taught you are born, die, and that is it. It is over. There is no coming back or reincarnation. Hopefully you go to Heaven.

And for non-believers or sinners they would go to a

horrifying place where there is total darkness and an eternal unquenchable fire. *

Although the Catholic Church does not believe in reincarnations, many early Christians did, until the Catholic Church banned it as a heretical offense.

The next day I made the appointment with the doctor Sylvia recommended. As the days grew closer I was apprehensive, though anxious, to meet this doctor in the hopes he could aid in confronting the demons that seemed to engulf me.

****

Dr. Tom was also an author of several books on regression and past lives. As soon as I met him I liked him for he was a soft-spoken, kind man.

For some reason I had an image in my mind of what he would look like---a short, nerdy man who wore bifocals and a crew cut.

I was pleasantly surprised when I walked in his office. He was sitting behind his desk and looked up displaying a sincere, warm smile.

He was a handsome older man who sported long gray hair he pulled back in a European ponytail.

We talked for at least an hour, covering many aspects of my life. When I told him about the experiences in Australia and continuing in my home he suggested one of his colleagues sit in on our next session.

When the hour was up, we made my second appointment for a week.

******

I found myself counting the days until I would see Dr. Tom again for I felt he would be the one to help me.

During the second session Dr. Tom was joined by a transcriber and an astrobiologist; someone who studies aliens. Dr. Tom told me he himself would be doing the hypnotizing. Seeing the frightened look on my face he explained hypnosis was nothing to fear--it is a form of harmonious communication —a natural trance state that can be triggered at any time by an individual possessing skills of induction and deepening.

He asked me if I had ever been hypnotized, so I told him about the incident in Las Vegas with the magician.

Dr. Tom drew the curtains and positioned me in a corner chair where I could hear the busy traffic outside the window, as it was now rush hour.

One moment I heard honking horns from irate drivers on the busy streets of Miami, and the next I saw myself laying on a cold, hard metallic table.

Out of my mouth came the words,
> *"Where am I?*
> *"Why am I naked?'*
> *"How did I get here?"*

From the corner of my eye I saw several shadows coming near me.

Although I tried to talk, the words would not come. In my mind I pleaded, *"Oh dear God. Please help me."*

Prompted by Dr. Tom I time traveled back to Australia

where I was sitting by the pool on a lounge chair talking to Michael when the sky suddenly turned black. Then we observed a shooting star, or meteorite, streak from one side of the sky to the other.

The next thing I saw was lying on a cold table, naked. I tried to move my body, but couldn't. The only thing I was able to move was my eyes. I blinked, hoping to find this was all just a bad dream and I would wake up any minute.

I tried to scream, opening my mouth to yell for help, but no words would come. It felt like I was in a sci-fi movie.

Suddenly I saw strange figures approach. Again, I tried to scream but it was useless.

At first I thought I was looking at a human being, but the skin on these creatures was whiter than mine. They were almost albino-like, stood around five feet tall and had blond hair. They resembled Asians and were very thin, weighing around 100 pounds.

There were five of them. Two were curvier so I assumed they were females.

I blinked, trying to get a closer look. When I did the one creature closest blinked back. I was conscious of screaming, "Please don't hurt me," but I sensed he couldn't hear me.

Although they were probing me everywhere, I felt no pain.

I noticed a huge metal implement stabilized in the ceiling above me begin to slowly descend. As it got closer, I saw it had a very pointed needle tip that was inching closer to my head.

When it reached me, I perceived the needle boring into

my head. I think that is when I must have passed out. The next thing I remember is looking up at the starlit sky alongside Michael.

Once again I heard horns outside the window and Dr. Tom counting backwards from ten. Now fully awake I saw the impassive faces of Dr. Tom and his colleague staring not at me, but through me.

The doctor played back the tape so I could hear what actually occurred that night in Australia. Would this be the answer that I needed to finally be at peace or was it just the opening of a new door?

******

After I was fully awake and able to understand what had just happened, Dr. Tom told me that this species of aliens called Pleiadians, also known as Nordic aliens, are the nicest and are concerned about the Earth and our future. They can travel between the third and ninth dimensions and all they really want to do is to help Earth and humanity ascend to higher dimensions.

There main concern is to help humans find their way through the higher planes of celestial knowledge and become more evolved. He said they are healers who are about peace and sharing.

They come from Pleiades (also known as the Seven Sisters) --a group of stars that are visibly from virtually every place that humanity inhabits Earth's globe.

This information did not make me feel any more at ease for if this really happened what did these creatures do to me that night? And the painting I was given by the Aboriginal women was of the Seven Sisters. What did all this mean?

******

After the hypnosis session I went to church and prayed to God to give me discernment and courage.

I now know that regression is a way that Satan has of making people move backwards in their walk with Jesus.

According to the Bible there is no coming back in another life after a person dies. The only one who was and ever will be resurrected was Jesus Christ the Son of God.

* Matthew 25:46 "And these will go away into eternal punishment, but the righteous into eternal life."

* Revelation 14:11 "And the smoke of their torment goes up forever and ever, these worshippers of the beast and its image, and whoever receives the mark of its name.

* Hebrews 6: "Therefore, leaving the elementary message about the Messiah, let us go on to maturity, not laying again the foundation of repentance from dead works, faith in God, teaching about ritual washings, laying of hands, the resurrection of the dead and eternal judgment.

* rationalwiki.org Pleiadians, also known as Nordic aliens are humanoid aliens that come from stellar systems surrounding the Pleiades stars. It is said they exist in the fifth dimension and want to help the earth and humanity

* Christiananswer.net The scriptures do not directly address the question of alien beings. The Bible does not inexplicitly confirm or deny the existence of intelligent life from other planets. Although the subject is not addressed explicitly, the Bible teaches implicitly the only thing God created with intelligence is the angels, man and animals.

13 A Confirmation

That particular time in my life was very troubling and perplexing. I questioned my sanity and all the things that had happened.

I was skittish and tense and others picked up on the sudden change in my demeanor. I had always been a very fun, loving, happy-go-lucky gal who people enjoyed being around. Now I was quiet, withdrawn and paranoid.

A few weeks after seeing Dr. Tom, my girlfriend April asked if I would like to take a trip to Aspen with her. She said she thought it would do me good to get away. I couldn't agree with her more and we left the next week.

I had never been to Aspen and didn't know how to ski but heard it was a beautiful place and quite a party town. Although I am not a fan of cold weather, I luckily still owned a fur coat and winter clothes from when I lived up north.

When we arrived in Aspen I could see why so many people visit and purchase vacation homes there. It really is spectacular and the town reminded me of a Monet painting

I once saw in an art gallery. It was beautiful and chic and you never know who you might see walking down the street.

The first day I saw Goldie Hawn, Kurt Russell, Mariah Carey and Jack Nicholson. I've always been a people watcher and seeing these celebrities close up was a thrill.

April and I hit all the hot spots and for a little while I had forgotten the bizarre experiences.

On the second day we took a ride on the Silver Queen Gondola to the top of Aspen Mountain.

Riding up the 11,212-foot summit we could see the entire town. There were hundreds of people skiing down the mountain, all dressed to the nines in their designer ski attire.

When we reached the top of the mountain we went to the Aspen Bar and Lounge-- the place where all the pretty people hung out.

Walking past the main bar I saw actor Michael Douglas and his gorgeous wife Katherine Zeta Jones.

As April and I were enjoying a hot toddy a man approached and introduced himself as Al, the Mayor of Aspen. He really wasn't the Mayor but was called that for he knew everyone in town.

Al invited us to his annual party, held at the swanky St. Regis Hotel, which ironically was taking place the following night. We accepted his offer and immediately went shopping to buy a new outfit. Not that we needed to but you know how women are----any excuse to buy something new.

******

As we walked into the Saint Regis, I was in awe at all the

beautiful people. Everyone who was anyone was enjoying a drink while mingling with friends.

Since Al had been a NASA space designer and inventor of a famous brand of basketball shoe, the theme to his soiree was for his guests to wear sneakers. Women were to dress in slinky ball gowns or mini dresses with a snazzy pair of tennis shoes and men, tuxedos with sneakers. Thus the party was called The Sneaker Ball.

After we were invited, I ran to a shoe store and bought a pair of high-heeled sneakers. I glued fur, glitter, and sequins on them-- nicely accentuating a form fitting mini dress I picked up at one of Aspen's chic boutiques.

Gracing the floor were famous actors, fashion models and executives who flew in on their private jets.

When Al spotted April and I he rushed over and made us feel at home, introducing us to many of his friends. Before long my girlfriend was surrounded by a bevy of single men all wanting to know who the 'pretty new face' in town was.

Seeing that she was going to be busy, Al and I went off to a quiet corner to get to know one another.

He was a brilliant man who at one time worked at NASA as an Apollo Program engineer and helped design the Moon Boot. He had won a number of awards for his work in space suit design, including NASA's Apollo Achievement Award for his contribution to man's first exploration of the Moon.

Al was one of the most fascinating, yet quirkiest men I had ever met.

I never knew anyone who had worked at NASA and was

quite impressed with the stories he told me. Perhaps that is why I began blurting out the Australia events.

I told him about my experience in the Olga's and the night I couldn't account 25 minutes of my life. After I was done, I was surprised at how easily I revealed my most intimate experiences to a complete stranger.

I was expecting him to laugh or look at me like I was a creature from outer space, but surprisingly he said, "Wow. That is so cool. And I know what you told me is exactly what happened to you!"

The next day Al took me to his house for he said he had something I had to see. As we walked in his office, there were dozens of boxes piled to the ceiling. He took one down marked "confidential," opened it, and brought out several sealed documents and pictures.

He said this was proof that not only do aliens exist, but that for decades the government has tried to conceal the fact that these beings have visited earth many times.

Over the years there have been many accounts of alien abductions. One in particular was reported by an Ashland, Nebraska police officer named Herbert Schirmer who claimed he was taken aboard a UFO in 1967 by humanoid beings with a slightly reptilian appearance." *

Al told me about the species known as 'hybrids'--- a mix between humans and the 'greys.' When he showed me a picture of what a hybrid looked like, my mouth dropped open.

"Vicki, what I am telling you is the truth and here in these boxes is the proof. The Hybrids are created by using DNA manipulation methods, as well as artificial insemination of abducted human victims."

I screamed, "God, no. I hope they didn't do anything to me! I had a partial hysterectomy years ago and they removed my uterus but left my ovaries."

He laughed again. "Who knows, there may be a little Vicki running around up there!"

But I didn't think it was so funny.

He told by me that the Pleiadians, also known as NORDIC ALIENS, resemble humans. However, they are highly advanced spiritual beings believed to exist in a different space-time dimension because of their ability to harness the powers of the higher spiritual planes.

I immediately thought about what Dr. Tom said about this species and it was exactly what Al was describing. Certainly two people who didn't know one another---one a brilliant doctor and the other a rocket scientist--- both acknowledging I had encountered Pleidians in Australia, was no coincidence.

Al said the species come from the stellar systems surrounding the Pleiades stars and can either switch between the third and the ninth dimension, or they exist solely in the fifth dimension.*

I thought to myself, "The fifth dimension? That's where Dr. J said I was brought into."

He said the Pleiadians' desire is to find the spiritual and mental powers in our world and are closely associated to the world light worker. *

"A light worker? Isn't that what Jane said I was."

Now I was seriously examining my sanity and mental health.

When I returned to the hotel I got down on my hands and knees and broke down sobbing. I prayed for God to help me get through this and if these bizarre events really had occurred, they were not demonic and I had not been in Satan's presence.

*Wikipedia

* Rationalwiki.org

* Pleiadians, also known as Nordic aliens are humanoid aliens that come from stellar systems surrounding the Pleiadas stars, It is said they exist in the fifth dimension and want to help earth and humanity.

Genesis 6:4 *Scripture speaks of demons penetrating the world physically by interbreeding with humans.*

14 The Jackie Gleason Room

After I left Aspen, I stayed in contact with Al.

As we said our goodbyes at the airport we made plans for him to visit me in Florida. He told me there was one more thing he thought might help me assess what happened in Australia, and it was located in Miami.

Three weeks later Al flew to Florida. I picked him up at the airport and we went somewhere quiet to have lunch.

He told me that the 1947 Roswell crash actually did occur and that two aliens who were on the craft survived the accident.

The military went to extreme measures to keep the entire incident quiet, covering up by saying it was merely a weather balloon that crashed called Project Mogul.

They located the aliens and whatever actually crashed into the disclosed area. Unfortunately, one of the creatures expired shortly after, but the second one survived and the President of the United States was brought in to observe the creature.

Al told me that actor/comedian Jackie Gleason was a good friend of the sitting President and the only civilian permitted to see the alien.

It was no secret that Gleason was into the occult and the paranormal especially UFO's, and the President had a similar fascination and shared the interest with Gleason.

Gleason was also a subscriber to the newsletter of the group of 'Just Cause' and amassed a collection of 1700 books on parapsychology, UFO's and the unknown. *

Al said that in 1973 President Nixon took Gleason to an air force base in Homestead. It was there that Nixon showed the comedian the dead alien body. When Gleason went home he told his wife Beverly that the creature he saw was small—about two-feet tall, had a baldhead and disproportionately large ears.

He also saw several containers that looked like "glass-topped Coke freezers." Inside the containers was what Gleason described as creatures looking like "mangled children," but under examination he discovered they were not humans at all and very old looking." *

After we were done eating, Al and I drove down to the University of Miami. He informed me that what I was about to see would solidify any doubts I still might have about my Australian experience.

******

Arriving at the University of Miami we were escorted to a room upstairs in one of the buildings. Standing by the door was a guard who stopped us from entering.

Al showed him the proper credentials verifying he was from NASA, which got us admittance. The room was a library that contained many wooden shelves filled with a vast collection of volumes of books, journals, periodicals, and publications in the field of parapsychology.

The materials consisted on the topics of witchcraft, ESP, UFO, reincarnation, mysticism and spiritualism. I had never seen such a large collection of paranormal books, pictures, and files in my life.

It truly was a life-long accomplishment of an individual who found the scholarly and popular literature of parapsychology a fascinating and entertaining subject

In 1988 after Jackie Gleason died, his wife Marilyn Gleason donated the massive collection to the University.

The next day Al returned to Aspen, but he will always remain in my heart.

Isaiah 47:10-14 *"For you have trusted in your wickedness. Therefore evil shall come upon you. Trouble shall fall upon you. Let now the astrologers, the stargazers and the monthly procrastinators stand up and save you from what shall come upon you."*

* The Presidents UFO website
* Wikipedia
* Presidentialufo.com

15 Sariel and Ariel

After my house sold I settled into a somewhat normal routine. I began going out with friends and tried to live a more simple life, for I longed for that tranquil feeling I had while staying with the Aboriginals.

One day while I was shopping at a new age/health food store admiring the section of non-allergenic fragrances, a light bulb went off in my head.

I asked the shop owner who was also a trained chemist if he could assist me in developing a spiritual fragrance.

Once again, I have no idea where that came from!

This was the year 2000 and spirituality paraphernalia was not nearly as prevalent as it is today.

Robert the chemist looked at me and said, "How in God's name did you come up with that?" I answered, "I have no idea, but I think this is what I was meant to do."

For the next year we worked feverishly to develop two fragrances--- one for a man and one for a woman.

The ingredients were all natural so people who had allergies would be able to wear it. The fragrances consisted of oils and herbs that have been used for centuries in healing, to gain wisdom, and to help us connect with nature such as: frankincense, sandalwood, cinnamon, vanilla, peppermint, sage and rose.

I named the fragrances after Archangels--- Sariel for the woman and Ariel for the man.

Ariel means lion or lioness of God and this archangel is associated with lions and animals. Ariel is also involved with healing and protecting nature—including animals, birds and fish, even the wild ones.

Sariel, also one of the seven archangels first appeared in the Book of Enoch. The name Sariel means "God's Command".

I spent most of the money I received in my divorce settlement to pay the chemist and package my perfume. Although my bank account had depleted to almost nothing, I still believed this was my calling in life.

I had a website designed and immediately started selling the perfume online getting orders from countries as far as India, China, Greece, and ironically Australia.

A few months after my business was up and running a Whole Life Wellness representative contacted me to be a guest speaker at their Fort Lauderdale Seminar. It appeared an employee had purchased my perfume and swore she felt healthier and calmer when wearing it.

******

I set up a booth at the Whole Life Seminar to sell my fragrances. I was pleasantly surprised the public was receptive and seemed to love the scents and the concept.

Although many people did not know what chakras were, the ones familiar with the energy centers were ecstatic that a fragrance was developed to help unblock and align them.

As I was speaking to the audience a man entered the room and sat in the front row. As our eyes met it was as if I had been struck by lightning for the physical attraction was nothing I had ever experienced before.

I thought to myself, "Is this what they mean by love at first sight?"

The man was not what you would call handsome and certainly not the 'pretty boy' type I was used to dating, but I couldn't take my eyes off of him. He was a rugged Charles Bronson type---a man's man.

When I was done with my speech the man walked up and introduced himself as Al. I thought to myself, "Another Al?" He told me he lived on a ranch in Montana and was visiting his sister in Florida.

As he took my hand and kissed it I thought to myself, "Oh no, here I go again!"

Matthew 5:28 *"But I say to you that everyone who looks at a woman with lustful intent has already committed adultery with her in his heart."*

16 Life on the Ranch

Throughout my travels I have encountered men from all walks of life. Some were rich, some poor, some were movie star handsome and others were on the plain side.

Looks had always been paramount to me and at that time in my life I never bothered to look at the inside of a man. I was always attracted to "the type of man my mother warned me about," and all that got me was trouble and heartache.

Both of my husbands were good looking. My second husband was much older as I was attracted to 'the older man'--the daddy figure.

When Al walked in the room my stomach began to flutter.

I thought to myself, "Here's the cowboy I've been waiting for all my life."

He strutted over to my booth with his snakeskin Tony Llama boots and purchased a case of my fragrance. He said he loved how it smelled and was very much into anything spiritual.

I turned to my girlfriend telling her perhaps I may have just met Mr. Right—the man I had been searching for all my life.

He certainly fit the bill. He was a cowboy who owned horses. He was good-looking in a rugged, bad boy sort of way, lived on a 750-acre ranch in Montana and was rich. What more could a girl ask for?

I gave Al my phone number and he called me that night.

Our first date took place a few nights later. We went to a nice Italian restaurant where we got to know each other very quickly.

He told me his wife had died ten years earlier in an automobile accident and he raised their three teenage daughters who were now grown and on their own.

Al was a retired New York contractor who was fifteen years my senior and a Catholic who attended church every day. By our third date we were madly in love, or maybe it was just madly in lust?

For the next three weeks Al and I saw each other every night. I couldn't believe I had only known this man for three weeks, for it felt like I knew him my entire life.

After the third week of dating Al invited me to Montana to visit his ranch. Although it was way too soon to go off gallivanting with someone I really didn't know, I didn't give it a second thought.

My mother wasn't happy about my decision to travel with a man I only knew for several weeks but at that time nobody could tell me anything. Once I made my mind up there was no changing it.

******

Al was an animal lover like I was--- dogs, cats, and lots of horses lived on his ranch. As we pulled up to the fifteen-foot gate that led onto the property my heart stopped beating.

Strategically placed on the 750 acres were three guest homes, one huge log cabin that served as the main house, a huge natural lake, multiple riding trails, a large barn, and a riding arena.

The ranch was impeccably manicured and looked like a picture on the front cover of Working Ranch Magazine. There were flowerpots lined along the road displaying colorful impatiens. Dozens of horses were grazing in the fields and in the far distance you could see herds of deer and buffalo soaking in the sun.

I thought I died and went to Heaven---literally.

******

After retiring at the age of fifty, Al became a world hunter who travelled the globe hunting every type of bighorn sheep. This didn't go over big with me for I loved animals and couldn't understand how anyone could shoot an innocent, beautiful animal just for the game of it. And if he was an animal lover how could he shoot them?

As I walked into his trophy room I was dumbfounded at how many eyes were staring down at me. Mounted on the walls were dozens of sheep heads.

I said to myself, "How in the heck am I ever going to live here?" But despite the glassy eyes peering at me, I quickly settled into country life.

We were so into one another and couldn't keep our hands to ourselves. When we went to a restaurant the waiter would say, "Why don't you two get a room?"

This behavior was not normal for me-- although I'm Italian and very affectionate, I do not display it with men in public.

That is, except with my cowboy, Al.

Several months after I moved on the ranch a major cosmetic company in New York contacted me inquiring about my fragrance. It appeared one of their employees heard me at the seminar and described my invention.

They asked me to fly to New York to consult about my unique product. Al flew with me and coached me on what to say and do and since he had been a very, very successful businessman, I appreciated his counsel.

On entering the office at the cosmetic company I requested the vice-president sign a non-disclosure form before I provided him the bottles of perfume. After the paper was signed by us both and notarized I handed him the two bottles—one for men and the other for women.

The executive said he liked the smell but LOVED the concept of 'aligning the chakras.' Then he asked me how much I wanted for my invention. I told him I didn't know for this was the ONLY spiritual perfume in the entire world.

And the fact that it consisted of all natural ingredients, made it even more valuable, for *everyone* could wear my perfume, even people who were allergic to most fragrances.

He suggested I hire a professional to plot out a forecast to determine it's worth. I thanked him and left.

When I returned to Montana I sought the proper counsel to help guide me. I recruited two men who came highly recommended and for the next several months they researched and finalized the forecast.

I called and made an appointment with the cosmetic company for the following month. The men I hired accompanied me to the meeting, suggesting we ask $1.5 million and 2% royalties.

At this meeting I met with the President of the company-- a cultured gentleman who listened to our presentation. He sat there quietly and on hearing the asking price he said, "Why would I give you a penny for this? My chemist is working on something like this right now."

I sat there in shock. After a few minutes of silence I said, "Sir, I have a non-disclosure signed by your Vice-President and if you copy my perfume, I will sue you."

He smirked stating, "Young lady, we are one of the largest cosmetic companies in the world. We have the best attorneys working for us and just MAYBE your great-great grandchildren will someday receive some money. That is, if you can afford to pay attorneys until then!"

I walked out of the office with my tail between my legs but my head held high. As soon as I got outside and saw Al I broke down in tears. Of course he felt horrible, but told me he had a surprise back at the ranch that would make me feel better.

Although I didn't say it out loud, I thought to myself that there was no gift that could mend my broken heart.

The next day we flew back to Montana.

******

By the time we got back to the ranch I settled down but still felt betrayed, conned and deceived by the major cosmetic company.

Al handed me a brown envelope, which contained two first class tickets to Africa. He said he was going to take me on my first Safari.

Then he had me close my eyes as he placed something in my hand. When I opened my eyes Al was on his knees and asked me to marry him.

Lying in my hand was the most beautiful five-carat diamond I had ever seen. The heartache and pain I felt from my New York business trip had dissipated. As he put the diamond on my finger he said, "You don't need to continue with your business. I will take care of you. I want you to be my wife. Will you marry me?"

I can't remember exactly what I said at the time, but I must have answered yes for we left for Africa the next week with a sparkling diamond ring on my finger.

John 4:17 *"Beloved, let us love one another, because love is from God; everyone who loves is born of God and knows God.*

Togo, Africa

17 A Ceremony Fit For A Queen

I've seen pictures of Africa in magazines but not one ever did the continent justice.

Al and I landed in Cape Town, South Africa, the land of Nelson Mandela, Shaka Zulu, and the famous Boer wars early in the morning. The sun was shining and the temperatures were rising.

There were so many beautiful things to see in Cape Town, such as the Victoria and Alfred Waterfront and The Kirstenbosch National Botanical Gardens.

With Africa's expansive landscapes and formidable animal life it is no wonder why millions of people visit there every year. I felt like I was in a place that hadn't changed for centuries.

After we left Cape Town we flew to Tanzania where thousands of wildebeest and several hundred thousand zebra make their annual migration yearly. There are tons of national parks in the country to see as well but the highlight for me was visiting the Stone Age Sites, some of which were up to 30,000 years old.

On our last day in Tanzania we went to the region of

Lake Victoria, which is the largest lake in Africa and the second freshwater lake in the world.

It was a beautiful sight as there are two rivers that flow out of the lake.

Al had a friend in the States, named Howard who was a powerful politician from Washington, D.C.

Being politically connected, Howard was friends with King Akew*, who ruled one of Africa's smaller countries.

When Howard heard we were going to Africa he asked if he could accompany us and made the arrangements for us to go on a private safari.

*The name has been changed for protection purposes

The next day we were picked up by a native named Abedemi, who drove us to where Al would hunt wildebeest and hartebeest. I still had a difficult time accepting the fact that slaying animals was acceptable, but after seeing the children in the village with ribs sticking out and belly buttons protrude, I prayed that Al was successful in his hunt for the meat would feed the children.

The country where King Akew reigned was a third world country that was underdeveloped and distressed. The streets were full of starving children begging for food. My heart went out to them and wanted to help in any way I could.

During the ride Abedemi explained that only the older or weak male animals were hunted and killed for the purpose of feeding their people. Even as animal domestication became relatively widespread, hunting was usually a significant contributor to the human food supply. And he assured me that if those selected animals were not shot, they would have to endure a slower, more painful death of being attacked and devoured by a stronger animal.

Although this was all so sad for I love animals so much I can't watch commercials where dogs are underfed or starving, I knew that a quick death for the weak prey would be better than hunted down by another animal and slowly eaten alive.

Abedemi drove us to a protected area where there were animals of many species, including zebras, elephants, wildebeest, springboks, and giraffes all running wild together.

Wading in the murky waters were hippos and crocodiles basking in the hot sun. It really was something to see.

I looked at Al and commented, "How can anyone question that there's a God?"

******

When I was introduced to the King I thought, "This is a King?" as he was nothing like I imagined him to look like.

He wore a long colorful gown and donned a silk turban. He appeared to be in his early forties and spoke perfect English.

King Akew was born, raised, and graduated from a university in America, but was elevated to the head of his Dynasty when his father, native to his country, passed away.

The king was highly respected and feared in his village and ruled his people with an iron fist.

One day while Al and I were having dinner with King Akew in his Palace, there was a knock on the door. A man from the village was escorted in, begging for the Kings forgiveness. It appeared the man's young son threw a rock and broke a window in someone's house.

King Akew sternly informed the child's father he would have to take responsibility for his actions and the punishment would be receiving twenty slashes.

I couldn't believe what I heard and without thinking blurted, "Don't you think that is too severe of a punishment for a child?"

The entire room went silent. Al kicked me under the table for nobody talks back or questions the King, I was later told.

Maybe it was the fact that I spoke up or maybe he just liked me, but the King invited us to be his guests at a ceremony that was to take place in the village the following day.

A statue of King Akew was being erected in his honor and Al and I were to be his special guests.

******

The next day when we arrived at the village, King Akew took my arm and told me I was about to witness how his people worshipped.

The entire village was there--- men, women and even

the small children. They had formed a circle and were praying and chanting.

As we neared the middle of the circle I heard a faint cry, which at first I thought was a baby.

As I looked ahead I saw two of the villagers holding a young lamb upside down by his small legs, while he struggled for freedom. The frightened animal had a wavering cry that mimicked a hungry infant.

The taller man took out a long, shiny blade and slashed the throat of the lamb. As the blood trickled from the animal the second man gathered the blood in a golden chalice that the King promptly drank from.

I couldn't believe what I was watching. I was sick to my stomach. I almost passed out and tried to cover my eyes. The King saw me and implied what I just witnessed was a great honor.

After King Akew drank the blood of the lamb, the villagers, including the children praised him. He told Al that his people sacrificed as they did in the days of Moses and animal sacrifice was still practiced in some traditional African religions.

I recalled reading in the Bible about the time when Moses came down from the mountain with the Ten Commandments. The Egyptian Jews were indulging in a pagan ceremony similar to what I had just observed, but I had no idea this sort of ritual was still being practiced.

After the lamb was slayed I begged Al to leave, but he said it was impossible for that would be disrespectful to the King. While trying to gather myself, I noticed Al and King Akew in deep conversation.

The next day we were brought back to the ceremonial area. I agreed to go only after my fiancé promised there would be no more animal worshipping.

When we arrived, all the villagers were waiting. The women wore dressed in tribal jewelry and colorful attire and the men were playing musical instruments and singing songs.

It was obvious that another type of ceremony was about to take place. I looked at Al and he said, "Don't worry, honey. This is going to be a happy celebration."

He took me by the hand and walked me to two beautiful jewel engrossed high-backed chairs, which were draped with lovely shiny material and donned with fragrant flowers. Al sat in one chair and I sat in the other.

A pair of elderly men I hadn't seen before approached us.

I looked at Al as he said, "I love you. This is our engagement ceremony, honey."

Just then several women brought over tall wooden sticks, which represented the power and life force. The King told Al and I we had to cross the sticks, which was part of the tradition.

The entire ceremony lasted about two hours.

There was wine and food for everyone. As I began eating I wondered if I was consuming the lamb that was killed the day before or the hartebeest Al shot on the safari.

I immediately put my plate aside saying I wasn't hungry.

When we finished our dinner King Akew came up behind us placing his hands on our heads as he recited something in his language. The entire village clapped and ran to congratulate us. I thought, "Thank you God for sending me my Prince."

The next week we returned to the States.

Proverbs 12:10 *Whoever is righteous has regard for the beast, but the mercy of the wicked is cruel*

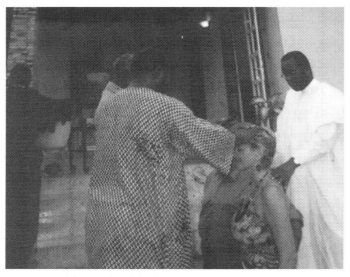

Being blessed by the King at our engagement party

18 ▸ Mr. Right Was Just Another Mr. Wrong

After returning to the States Al and I resumed life on the ranch. We were so in love and I couldn't wait to be his wife.

We set a date for our wedding, which would take place on my mother's birthday, July 4, the following year. We started making plans, which included flying our families and closest friends to the ranch.

As the months flew by I counted the days until I would say, "I do." Although I was deliriously in love, that nagging emptiness I had endured throughout my life once again throbbed inside me.

I asked God, "What am I missing in my life? Please God show me the answer. You have given me everything a woman could possibly want and I am grateful, but there is still an emptiness inside that nothing can seem to fill."

One day while we were lying in bed Al asked what I wanted for my engagement present. After thinking long and hard I said I would like a life size replica of Jesus Christ on the cross, carved out of wood that we could erect on the ranch.

The next day Al contacted a wood carver in the area who was known for doing the best work.

The three of us began visiting churches, meeting with several priests to make sure we had the precise measurements, details, and facts.

The only problem we encountered was whether the nails driven into Christ were in His wrists or His hands.

The consensus was they were driven into His hands for if they were nailed into His wrists it could not have supported His weight. Just thinking about the unbearable pain that Jesus endured for us made my heart ache.

******

The next several months Al and I were busy making wedding plans and checking on our wooden cross that was coming along nicely. We planned on cementing the six-foot plus wooden structure by a fresh water stream that ran along the ranch. This way it could be viewed from the main house and pretty much the entire ranch.

Once the cross was placed in the ground I was going to plant a garden of colorful flowers around the base and place a bench at the foot where we could sit and pray daily.

My life would soon be complete. I was living a fairy tale and the ending would be 'happily ever after' by my marrying my Prince. Although it was exactly what I had dreamed of and hoped for, that vacant space remained in my heart.

I asked myself over and over again, "What is missing?"

After all, I had certainly been blessed in my life. God had given me everything a person could possibly want, and more. Much more. So why did I feel like there was something missing?

******

Eight months before our wedding was to take place I received a phone call from my son in Florida. He had dropped out of school and was severely depressed.

I told Al that I had to fly there to see what the problem was.

Upon arrival I discovered Joey had broken up with his girlfriend and spiraled into a severe depression. I tried to talk to him and cheer him up but discovered that my absence the past year had him feeling lonely and deserted.

We had always been very close like my mother and I, and my long distance living arrangement had taken its toll on him.

Although I didn't realize it at that time, I now see I was selfish in thinking about my happiness and not considering my son or mothers feelings.

******

It was the week before Thanksgiving when I flew back to Florida. The following week Al followed.

He walked into my house and told me how much he loved and missed me and didn't want to be away from me another day.

As we were talking my son walked in the room and said hello to Al.

Without even acknowledging him, Al told him he came to take me to the ranch for Thanksgiving was coming up and he always threw an annual Thanksgiving soiree.

My son replied, "My grandmother is coming to Florida to spend Thanksgiving with me and mom, like she always does. Maybe you would like to join us?"

Before I could say anything Al snapped, "Your mother is mine now." He turned to me and said, "You have to choose. It's me or your son."

I didn't know if I heard him correctly.

He couldn't possibly have asked me to choose between him and my son, could he? Not this 'perfect' man I had been waiting all my life for!

I looked at Al and said, "That isn't funny. You are kidding, right?"

Once again he replied, "It's me or your son."

I handed Al back the engagement ring for it was now just a shiny piece of glass. Once again, I had chosen Mr. Wrong.

Heartbroken, I said goodbye to Al and remained in Florida with my son. Although I missed him very much I knew that any man who truly loved a woman would not ask her to choose between him and her child.

Yes, I was depressed for I am human. I remained in my house for months refusing to socialize with anyone. I prayed to God to give me strength and to heal my heart. I begged him to show me what it was He wanted me to do, but unfortunately it would be a few more years and heartaches before He would reveal the answer.

Matthew 22:29 *But Jesus answered them, "You are wrong, because you know neither the Scriptures nor the power of God."*

The cross we had built.

19 ⟩ A Medical Mistake

I never heard from Al again. Eventually I picked myself up and tried to resume a somewhat normal life. I started going out with my friends and met many men, but in my eyes nobody could replace Al.

But replace what? A man who was making me choose between him and my only child?

Thank God for my mother. Every year she would drive to Florida and spend winters with Joey and me, which was what I needed. In the summer I would fly up north to her and stay a week.

My mom had always been my best friend and #1 fan. No matter what I did, I could do no wrong. And Joey was her only grandchild so she doted on him until the day God took her home.

******

Mom was petrified of doctors and refused to go to one; thus she never had yearly physicals or went to a dentist.

When I visited her I'd watch her dogs so she could go to Atlantic City for a few days with a senior citizen group.

It was the only thing she did, so I was glad to give her the opportunity to get away and relax.

One night in February while mom was with me in Florida, Joey woke me and asked where the closest hospital was. He said mom was in severe pain and needed to go to the ER.

I wanted to drive her but she wanted Joey to take her so I could stay with her two dogs. She was obsessed with her animals and wouldn't leave them for a minute unless I stayed with them.

She didn't appear to be in severe pain and said she thought it was just a bad stomachache. When Joey returned home at 6 AM alone I threw my clothes on and drove to the hospital. When I walked in her room the doctor was asking her when was the last time she saw a dentist. She told him it had been at least 20 years.

A second doctor came in several hours later saying the x-ray showed a piece of mom's dental bridge had broken off and was lodged in her small bowel.

She then admitted that several years before on one of her trips to Atlantic City, she bit into a steak and swallowed the tooth. She didn't tell anyone because she thought she would 'pass it' and was afraid to go to a hospital.

If only she would have told someone then!

For the next twenty-eight days I had to watch a perfectly healthy seventy-four years young woman slowly die before me.

What's ironic is my mom was petrified of hospitals and her biggest fear was to have to go to one in Florida.

People say that hospitals kill you---especially in Florida--- for there's so many elderly people that of course the statistics of people dying in hospitals are higher there.

It turned out mom's dental plate broke off that night in Atlantic City and God knows how long it was lodged in her body.

That particular night at my house I had baked caramelized walnuts. The doctor said the hard nuts dislodged the piece and pushed it down to her bowel. Unfortunately, it would not pass through.

They performed a colonoscopy that should have solved the problem, but after several hours the surgeon came out, saying he couldn't grab the piece.

By now my mom was a wreck and although I had a poker face assuring her everything was going to be okay, I sensed this was not going to end well.

When the second surgeon who was going to remove the piece arthroscopically saw me in tears he coldly said, "What are you crying for? I'll tell you when its time to cry!"

That should have been a sign for me to take mom out of there, but this hospital had great ratings and the surgeon was said to be their best.

The second procedure was performed and I assured mom she would be fine.

The next morning when I went into mom's room a nurse was attending to her and they were cleaning the floor. I was told mom had a bad night, for someone went in and mistakenly fed her a chicken dinner!

It was clearly marked on her door, "no food and no water," because of the surgery, but the aid either didn't bother to read or ignored it.

Mom ate the food and aspirated, launching what they called a "comedy of horrors." I watched helpless as my mother slowly died in front of me, filling up with septic poison.

After the third week I called a friend of ours--- a Catholic priest that had known our family for decades (In fact, he married me and my first husband, Joe) who lived not far away. He came to the hospital and gave mom her last rights.

I'll never forget that day. Although she was in a semi-coma, when Father said Amen, mom tried raising her hands up (they were tied to the bed because she kept trying to take the tube out of her mouth).

I crawled in bed with her for the doctor said she would be dead in 15 minutes. Well her heart was strong and she held on for three long hours. I found it ironic that she died at 3 PM --the same time Jesus died on the cross.

Right before she took her last breath, I told her it was okay to go for I would take care of Joey, my sister Karen, and her beloved dogs. I said her mother was waiting for her and the angels were coming to take her.

She squinted, opening her eyes, looked up and smiled. Then she died.

Although I knew this was coming, I didn't want to let go.

One of the ironic things is that mom loved her dog, Samantha so much she always said she wanted to die before Sammie did.

Samantha had diabetes and had to be given shots twice

a day. That month mom was in the hospital I would come home to the dogs and fall apart, crying myself to sleep.

Dogs are very smart and perceptive and Sammie knew something was very wrong since mom wasn't there and went into a depression refusing to eat.

Three days after my mother died, Sammie died in my arms. It was as if mom took Sam with her. Moms wish was to be cremated, so I cremated the dog and they are buried together.

Whether this was a coincidence or and act of God, I can't say, but mom got her wish and is with her four-legged daughter.

******

After mom's death a lot of things surfaced. Four mistakes had occurred in the hospital that were total negligent. First, when they tried to remove the piece of dental plate the first day the surgeon punctured her bowel.

Second, the second surgeon (the one who told me "I'll tell you when its time to cry") didn't securely suture her, thus poison started leaking.

Third, the aide fed her right after the operation. Fourth, a few days before mom passed I walked in to ICU and discovered she was filling up with more poison due to the fact that 'the kidney machine' had broke and they didn't have another machine at the time. (Her stomach was distended like a huge balloon).

I confronted the first surgeon as to why mom was not getting better and he said, "It's not my mistake, it's the other surgeons."

After she died I called for an inquisition, which of course

the doctors did not attend. I discovered there was nothing I could do for Florida is a state that 'protects' the malpractice performed by the doctors.

I hired a lawyer on the other coast who came highly recommended. I called and told him what happened. He said, "this was a $25 million dollar case, and that he could not bring mom back but justice would be done."

Then he asked if I, and her other children were over 25. He informed me since mom was divorced and not married and her children were over 25, there was no case.

I thought he was kidding, but sadly discovered that if a person dies in Florida from malpractice and is single and their children are over 25, there is nothing anyone can do. This law was enforced to protect the amount of malpractice for there are many people who fit in that category living there.

I had mom cremated and kept her ashes with me until I could drive back home to Pittsburgh and bury her alongside her parents.

I was very depressed and bitter. I was mad at God for taking a perfectly healthy woman for no reason. Why? I kept asking Him.

Revelation 14:13 *"Then I heard a voice from heaven say, "Write this: Blessed are the dead who die in the Lord from now on." "Yes," says the Spirit, "they will rest from their labor, for their deeds will follow them."*

20 Supernatural Events

The next few weeks I walked around in a fog. I was heartbroken and distraught and cried constantly questioning God why He took my mom.

My son who was close to his grandmother was also devastated but tried to be there for me, for now it was just the two of us.

I made arrangements to drive to Pittsburgh and let my Aunt (mom's sister) keep the urn for awhile for the two of them were extremely close and she also was bitter, sad and confused why this tragedy happened.

After driving twenty hours, Joey and I arrived at moms house. We found it just the way she left it every year when she came to Florida. She would disconnect the phone service, turn the electric to a moderate temperature so the pipes would not freeze, and have the mail re-directed to my house.

When we unlocked the front door the phone began to ring. We stopped and looked at one another for the phone was on the floor with the cord pulled out of the wall, wrapped around it.

Joey turned white and asked, "Mom what's happening? How can the phone be ringing? It's not connected."

Instinctively I answered, "It's nana. She wants us to know she's okay."

To this day, I have no logical answer how that phone rang, but it did!"

I took the urn to my aunts and she placed it on top of a table in her upstairs hallway. It seemed to give her solace knowing that her sister was near.

******

The first strange thing that happened was on the very first night. The day after dropping the urn off, my aunt called me saying she had a dream that mom was calling out to her. My aunt said, "Viv, where are you? I can't see you."

Aunt said mom answered, "I'm in room 341." My aunt called their brother who told his wife who played the numbers. She bet that number straight and guess what! That night the number 341 came in!

Coincidence or???

As if that wasn't enough for a skeptic to start believing, my aunt who was the straightest person began experiencing eerie events that even freaked her out.

She kept a picture of mom riding an electrical bull on top of her television in the living room. At that time my aunt was watching her great-nephew for her niece.

One day she went from the living room to the kitchen. When she returned to the living room, the box of diapers were scattered across the floor. There was nobody else in the house and the baby was not big enough to grab it and toss it.

Next, my aunt would be watching television and mom's picture would fly off the television to the floor.

Trying to make sense of these strange occurrences the last straw that sent Aunt over the edge was at night when she was sleeping.

She slept on the couch downstairs and would be awoken by water running in the bathroom upstairs. She would go up there and find the water running in the sink. This happened for three nights in a row.

She knew she didn't leave it running and there was nobody else in her house so she called me up crying, "Please come get your mother and let's bury her."

My aunt was freaked out and believed that mom was not at peace and wanted to be buried alongside her parents.

We had a small burial, placing the urn next to her parents and the events immediately ceased.

Phillipians 4:13 *"I can do everything through him who gives me strength."*

21 Getting Baptized in the Ocean

After we buried my mother I tried to resume a somewhat normal life.

What happened in Australia and the sudden and senseless death of my mother had me questioning God.

Why would He take a young, healthy woman when she had years more to live? But who was I to ask God that?

I became more bitter and angry so I started attending Catholic mass every morning and receiving communion hoping that would help.

Although I felt better while I was in church, my mind would race and my stomach would churn as soon as I left.

One day a friend asked me to go with her to her church—an evangelical church called Calvary Chapel.

At first I felt a little uncomfortable for their worship was so different than what I was used to.

Everyone was very nice and welcomed me with open arms. They sang along with the wonderful choir provided.

After a few weeks I found myself letting my hair down and joining them in praising God. I would raise my arms and break down crying every time I went for something would come over me.

The bitterness began to subside and questioning of my mom's death began to make more sense.

I talked to several people who informed me that was mom's time and place to die. No matter what I did, or didn't do, her number was up.

We all make plans for the future—where we want to be---where we want to go--- and yet we are not in control. When we are born God knows the date, time and place when we will die.

No matter how good you take care of yourself, eating healthy and exercising, when your number's up, it's up!

I've known people who were heath nuts and fitness gurus who didn't smoke, drink and ate healthy.

One had a fatal heart attack and the other who never smoked died of lung cancer.

One Sunday I heard the pastor talking about being baptized or re-baptized in the ocean. Those interested were meeting the following week for 'baptism at the beach' at Pompano Beach.

Although I had been baptized when I was a week old, this would be my chance to show my faith to God that I am a believer.

The pastor emphasized that being baptized as an infant was our parents' commitment to God and this would be an expression of our adult commitment to Christ.

On October 8, 2011, I went with my girlfriend and her

son to Pompano Beach. I was shocked to find hundreds of people waiting to dedicate their life to the Lord.

The pastor had several elders with him explaining that being baptized would not 'save' us, for only your faith in Christ could do that.

He said that Baptism is a public declaration that you are identifying yourself with Christ our Savior. Baptism symbolizes an individual's identification with God, Christ, and His people. The new relationship is based on God's grace through one's faith in Christ's finished work on the cross.

When it was my time, I walked into the warm salt water and was gently lowered under the waves.

I'm not sure what I was expecting--- for the skies to open as it did when John the Baptist baptized Jesus or what, but of course nothing like that happened.

The only thing I do know is that I felt like a new person as my head came out of the water. I felt cleansed and reborn.

I went home that day, expecting my life to be perfect now and live each day in peace. But of course that didn't happen, for the devil would not let go.

Acts 2:38 *And Peter said to them, "Repent and be baptized every one of you in the name of Jesus Christ for the forgiveness of your sins, and you will receive the gift of the Holy Spirit."*

22   Chastened and Humbled

After my baptism I thought my life would run smoothly. Since I showed God that I was willing to dedicate my life to Him, He would finally send me 'Mr. Right,' I would have no financial problems, and live in perfect peace and harmony.

WRONG! You see, God has a funny sense of humor and it does not matter what we want, wish, or hope for.

We can think we are in control and make plans that most likely will never happen.

My mom always said I lived in a fairy tale world. Thus it opened doors to disappointment and heartaches.

******

The next few years I met several men thinking maybe they would be 'the one,' only to discover they were all Mr. Wrongs.

I'm not saying they were bad men—they were all nice--but just not the one for me.

My finances went from bad to worse for my ex-husband declared bankruptcy, which ceased my lifetime alimony. I was so stressed, worrying about how I would be able to support myself, for everything I had done in my younger years I could not do now. I was too old to model and train horses.

One day I was contacted by an oil and gas company who wanted to lease my rights. This was on land that John and I bought in Pennsylvania while we were married. When we sold it, we maintained the gas and mineral rights and John turned the rights over to me, if we were ever to divorce.

I flew to Pennsylvania and met both my divorce lawyer and representative from the oil company. He wrote me a hefty check and said I would receive annual checks that would financially set me for life. But as quickly as this blessing occurred, it would be three long years before it was taken away.

Since my husband owed millions to the bank due to his automobile business out of trust, the bankruptcy court fought me stating that I didn't legally own the rights for the deed was never recorded. After three years of fighting and lawyers bills, I not only lost what was mine, but it cost be tens of thousands to pay the attorney!

Having no career to fall back on and now in my fifties, I needed a job. I applied at retail stores, restaurants, and everywhere I could, but nobody would hire me, either saying I had no experience or most likely because I was too old.

Out of desperation I began to write books. I wrote about relationships, self-help, for children, horse-related and spiritual.

I published my work with a renowned Christian publisher who eventually went belly up taking the authors money and leaving us in the cold.

I sought another publisher and decided to write a sexy, racy novel for it seemed that was what people wanted to read. While writing it, although I tried to do it in a positive way, it still talked about same sex marriage, explicit sex acts, and things that God did not approve of.

The book took off and I appeared on a national television show. An actor's mother contacted me for she was interested in making it into a movie.

Finally! All those years of writing, getting screwed by the publisher and the money it cost to publish would pay off! I told myself this was the big one---the one I have been waiting for all my life.

I hired a PR firm out in California who set up a meeting with a Hollywood producer. As I was packing and getting ready to fly out west I woke in a cold sweat, gasping for air.

Passing it off as a panic attack, I ignored it. The next morning I would have an awakening that would change my life.

Proverbs 13:24 *He who spares his rod hates his son. But he who loves him disciplines him promptly.*

23   Winning the Battle Against Satan

Every day I thank God my son was staying at my house on May 1, 2018. Joey was living with with me due to the fact that several months earlier I began having excruciating pains in my groin. I went to an orthopedic surgeon and after taking ex-rays they discovered I had severe osteoarthritis in both hips.

It came as a shock because up until that time, I had no warning. I was very active, exercising and working with my horses.

Questioning the diagnosis I went to another surgeon for a second opinion. That surgeon confirmed that yes indeed I was bone-on-one in both hips and would need them replaced.

I was a healthy sixty-three years young woman who was pretty fit so finding out I needed to have both hips replaced came as a shock to myself and all those who knew me.

Being I had to wait a year and a half until being eligible for Medicare and not able to afford the costly operations, I decided to have my hips injected with cortisone. I knew the cortisone injections helped my racehorses for they would be lame one day and after injected with the chemical they would miraculously be pain-free for several months.

The surgeon agreed the shots should help me and hopefully I would be able to delay the operation until I came of age to collect financial help.

I found a reputable pain management doctor who injected both hips with the aid of a fluoroscope. After several days my right hip was pain free, but my left was still hurting.

Two weeks later the doctor re-injected my left side thinking this would do the job.

Several mornings later I woke and couldn't put any weight on that leg. Over the next few days, it worsened.

I became dependent on a walker to move about and was immobile. The pain was excruciating but told they could not operate until the cortisone dissipated (which would take at least three months).

I hobbled around-- bitter and mad for my life had done a complete turn. I became a prisoner in my home and depended on everyone to do the simple things we take for granted such as drive a car, go to the grocery and just walk.

I couldn't even walk my dog and had to rely on neighbors and friends.

My trip to Hollywood was put on hold and any promoting for the book had to wait until I had the operation and could walk.

One day I fell in my house. I didn't think a thing about it, but the pain worsened.

Only a few weeks before the operation was to take place, I woke at 4 AM gasping for air. I ignored it thinking it was just another panic attack until the next morning when I woke and felt like someone was sitting on my chest.

I told my son to call my friend, Bob, for I needed to go to the hospital. I knew Joey was freaked and scared and thought Bob would help both of us feel more at ease.

When we arrived at the hospital they put me in a room where the doctor on call started checking my vitals and doing tests. He was concerned that my oxygen level was quite low—it was 85 when normal is 100—so they began administering oxygen.

The tests came back normal so the baffled doctor ordered one last test. When those results came back, I was rushed to ICU where they informed me I had a 'saddle double pulmonary embolism.' There were two blood clots on my lungs---one being 'massive' and was pushing on my heart.

Knowing nothing about these medical terms, I didn't understand the severity and danger I was in.

Thank God I was too ignorant to understand the danger I was in for I might have died from stress and nerves. They performed a procedure to dissolve the clots and sent me back to ICU.

The next morning I was taken back to the operating room where a surgeon said they had to implant an IVC filter in a vein in my stomach.

At first I argued and would not sign the consent form. It was Deja Vu, for this was the same hospital my mom had died in from medical errors. And she died because of a foreign object inside her (or trying to remove it) and now they wanted to implant a device in me.

The surgeon informed me if I was going to have hip

operations, I must have the filter for it would catch any clots that were still in me or could come from the operation.

I signed the form and they implanted it.

I remained in the hospital for four days. The doctor told my son I had a 50/50 chance of living. At that time I had no idea how many people die from pulmonary embolisms every year, and I had two—one being massive!

Today I'm sitting here writing this book while waiting for the first operation to take place. I'm down to four weeks. I'm stuck at home with all the time in the world to think. And that's a dangerous thing!!

I'm not angry, but scared to death, questioning God why this is happening to me. I realize this could be worse and He allowed me to live for a reason. I have always believed that 'things happen for a reason' but for the life of me I couldn't figure out why.

Praying and praying about it, God told me to write my biography, but I mustn't hold anything back and be 100 % honest.

When I told my crazy life story to people they would say, "You have to write a book." But I was hesitant---afraid that people would question some of the events, criticize me and question my credibility.

I'm not special but my life story is definitely different than most.

The story I have just told is true and the bizarre events really did happen.

I still don't know exactly what happened to me the night I lost 25 minutes in Australia? Had I been abducted?

Are there really creatures called Plaeidians? Were the events demonic and evil and I am blessed to have come out of it alive as a child of God?

Although the subject of life on other planets is not addressed clearly the Bible teaches implicitly that the only things God created with intelligence are the angels, man, and animal.

I have finally won my personal battle against Satan. I know he will never leave me alone. As long as I continue my walk with God, the devil will pursue bringing me heartache, health and financial problems.

I still have trouble believing those things happened in Australia, but they did. Since I have months waiting for my operation, the rehabilitation period, and healing, I have all the time in the world to thank God for saving me and glorify Him.

My story can belong to one of many women who have experienced something like I have. There are many people–both men and women, who spend their entire life searching for that special person or thing to bring them happiness.

They slave to attain the riches they think they deserve–no matter what price they have to pay. Some even go as far as selling their soul to the devil himself.

Through it all I discovered that the wealthiest and most celebrated people leave the world the same way as the not so fortunate. Nobody has ever towed his riches behind him in a hearse.

Many are searching for their 'soul mate'– that one true love, but unfortunately most never find him or her.

Ironically, I spent my entire life looking for Mr. Right when all along He was right next to me. He never once left me— in sickness, pain, or heartbreak.

I was just looking at the wrong things and putting my trust in people.

I recently signed up for an on-line college course where I'm studying for a doctorate in ministry. My life has done a complete turnaround. I tell people God knocked me off my horse to humble me. He taught me to look and appreciate the simple things in life such as the ocean, the birds, and to live a simple life.

I once had it all--- fame, money, and a life one only dreams of, but nothing and nobody could ever make me happy. Jesus had to slow me down----and boy did He---- to show me what really matters in life. Whatever time I have left in this world will be to serve the Lord. If I helped one person with my story, it was worth it.

If Christ chooses to send me someone to grow old (er) with, He will. It will not be on my terms as it had been before for He knows what is good for me and for you. We just have to take the time to be still and listen.

Remember, Satan will test and tempt you until the day you are called back to your Heavenly home as he does to me. Faith---that's one of the hardest things a person will have to learn in their life for you must believe in something and someone. Faith is the backbone of Christianity that strengthens your walk with Jesus Christ.

It is designed as belief with strong conviction, reliance or devotion. We have to put our trust in someone, so why not Christ?

Update. I have had the first operation, which was successful. The second will be performed in four months. The surgeon told my son that he has no idea how I walked at all for when he opened me up there was nothing at all there. The hip joint had deteriorated and crumbled into dust.

The very same day I was up walking. This is truly a miracle and I am positive now that God kept me here to tell you this story. He is in control and will never leave us.

ABOUT THE AUTHOR

Victoria M. Howard has written eighteen books. Her work has been published in the New York Times, The Paulick Report and many other magazines and papers. She has appeared on Fox & Friends, The Morning Blend, Good Morning Sacramento, and Good Day L.A.

Victoria once hosted a radio show called Beauty and the Shrink and penned the relationship column, Dear Victoria.

In 2017 she was inducted into the Harness Racing Hall of Fame in Florida for her literary works.

She has owned, bred, and trained standardbreds for forty years and lives in Florida with her dog, Max.

Printed in the United States
By Bookmasters